CONTEXTS OF BEING
*The Intersubjective Foundations
of Psychological Life*

Psychoanalytic Inquiry Book Series

Volume 12

Psychoanalytic Inquiry Book Series

CONTEXTS OF BEING
The Intersubjective Foundations
of Psychological Life

ROBERT D. STOLOROW
GEORGE E. ATWOOD

THE ANALYTIC PRESS

1992   Hillsdale, NJ   London

Published by The Analytic Press, Inc.
365 Broadway, Hillsdale, NJ 07642

Typeset in Schneidler by Lind Graphics, Upper Saddle River, NJ

Library of Congress Cataloging-in-Publication Data

Stolorow, Robert D.
    Contexts of being : the intersubjective foundations of
psychological life / Robert D. Stolorow, George E. Atwood.
        p. cm. – (Psychoanalytic inquiry book series ; v. 12)
    Includes bibliographical references and index.
    ISBN 0-88163-152-3
    1. Psychoanalysis. 2. Intersubjectivity. 3. Psychotherapist and
patient. I. Atwood, George E. II. Title. III. Series.
    [DNLM: 1. Psychoanalytic Theory. 2. Psychoanalytic Therapy. W1
PS427F v. 12]
    RC506.S738 1992
    616.89'17 – dc20
    DNLM/DLC
    for Library of Congress   92-21982
                                                                   CIP

Printed in the United States of America
10 9 8 7 6 5 4 3 2

To the memory of Dede

i am through you so i. — *e. e. cummings*
Through the *Thou* a man becomes *I*. — *Martin Buber*
There is no such thing as an infant. — *D. W. Winnicott*

Contents

Preface

THAT THIS BOOK WOULD NOT HAVE BEEN WRITTEN were it not for
the late Daphne Stolorow – Dede, as she was called by her
loved ones and friends – is a statement that holds true in many
ways. Her unfailing love, boundless devotion, and enthusiastic
encouragement were the medium that for eight years nourished
her husband's creativity and courage to articulate himself.
"You're *so* provocative," she would often say to him, with an
approving twinkle in her eye. This book was conceived in the
wake of her death. We drew closer and decided to try to create
something lasting from the ashes of loss and sorrow.

Despite her youth – she was only 34 when she died – Dede
was already showing her brilliance as a psychoanalytic thinker.
Her vibrantly active mind lives on in many of the pages of this
book. She was the senior author of the original article (Stolorow
and Stolorow, 1989) that formed the basis for chapter 5. Her
ideas on affect integration and its derailment, originally published in another article of which she was senior author (Socarides and Stolorow, 1984/85), were centrally important in the
development of chapters 2, 3, and, especially, 4. Dede's dear
friend Sheila Namir also made major contributions to the development of the ideas in chapter 4 – her tribute to Dede and gift to
Dede's husband. We all miss you, Dede, deeply.

Bernard Brandchaft coauthored chapter 6, but the influence of his thinking permeates the entire book. During the nearly 15 years of our collaboration with him, he has contributed so much to the evolution of intersubjectivity theory that it would be impossible to do justice to his impact in shaping this framework. Jeffrey Trop coauthored chapter 7 and lent his enthusiasm to the entire project.

We are deeply grateful to Elizabeth Atwood, who has actively supported our collaboration throughout its long history and who sustained us both during the summer of 1991 when we outlined this book at a cabin on Rangeley Lake in Maine. We are indebted as well to Elena Bonn, whose love and encouragement have also been vital to the completion of this work.

We wish to thank Lawrence Erlbaum and Joseph Lichtenberg for their support of this project, Paul Stepansky for his valuable editorial guidance, and Eleanor Starke Kobrin for her excellent copy editing.

Some of the material in this book was originally published elsewhere.

Several paragraphs in the section on "The Ontogeny of Personal Experience" in chapter 1 appeared in *Psychoanalytic Inquiry* (1991, 11:171–184) and in *The Relational Self,* ed. R. Curtis (New York: Guilford Press, 1991, pp. 17–33).

Portions of chapter 2 appeared in *Psychoanalytic Inquiry* (1989, 9:364–374) and in *The Psychoanalytic Review* (1992, 79:25–30).

An earlier version of chapter 3 appeared in *Psychoanalytic Dialogues* (1991, 1:181–195).

Portions of chapter 5 appeared in *Psychoanalytic Inquiry* (1989, 9:364–374) and in *The International Journal of Psycho-Analysis* (1989, 70:315–326).

An earlier version of chapter 6 appeared in *The Annual of Psychoanalysis* (1990, 18:99–114).

An earlier version of chapter 7 appeared in *Contemporary Psychoanalysis* (1989, 25:554–573) and one of the case studies also appeared in *The Relational Self,* ed. R. Curtis (New York: Guilford Press, 1991, pp. 17–33).

We thank the editors and publishers of these journals and books for giving us permission to include this material in our book.

Introduction

This book is the culmination of some 20 years of collaborative work elaborating what we have come to call the intersubjective perspective in psychoanalysis. Intersubjectivity theory is a field theory or systems theory in that it seeks to comprehend psychological phenomena not as products of isolated intrapsychic mechanisms, but as forming at the interface of reciprocally interacting subjectivities. Psychological phenomena, we have repeatedly emphasized, "cannot be understood apart from the intersubjective contexts in which they take form" (Atwood and Stolorow, 1984, p. 64). It is not the isolated individual mind, we have argued, but the larger system created by the mutual interplay between the subjective worlds of patient and analyst, or of child and caregiver, that constitutes the proper domain of psychoanalytic inquiry. From this perspective, as we shall see, the concept of an individual mind or psyche is itself a psychological product crystalizing from within a nexus of intersubjective relatedness and serving specific psychological functions.

Early germs of the theory of intersubjectivity can be found in a series of psychobiographical studies in which we explored the personal, subjective origins of the theoretical systems of Freud, Jung, Reich, and Rank. From these studies, which formed the basis of our first book *Faces in a Cloud* (Stolorow and Atwood, 1979), we concluded that, since psychological theories derive to a significant degree from the subjective concerns of their creators, what psychoanalysis needs is a theory of subjectivity itself—a unifying framework that can account not only for the phenomena that other theories address but also for these theories themselves. We outlined a set of skeletal proposals for the creation of such a framework, which we envisioned as a depth psychology of human experience, purified of the mechanistic reifications of Freudian metapsychology. Our initial framework took the "representational world" of the individual as its central theoretical construct, picturing this world as evolving organically from the person's encounter with the critical formative experiences that constitute his unique life history. Later (Atwood and Stolorow, 1984) we dropped the term "representational world" because we became aware that it was being used to refer both to the imagistic *contents* of experience and to the *thematic structuring* of experience. Hence, we decided to use "subjective world" when describing the contents of experience and "structures of subjectivity" to designate the invariant principles unconsciously and recurrently organizing those contents according to distinctive meanings and themes.

Although the concept of *inter*subjectivity was not introduced in *Faces in a Cloud*, it was clearly implicit in the demonstrations of how the subjective world of a psychological theorist influences his understanding of other persons' experiences. Indeed, the book's central theme was captured in the phrase, "the observer is the observed" (p. 17). The first explicit use of the term "intersubjective" in our work appeared in an article (Stolorow, Atwood, and Ross, 1978) in which we conceptualized the interplay between transference and countertransference in psychoanalytic treatment as an intersubjective process reflecting the interaction between the differently organized subjective worlds of patient and analyst. Foreshadowing much work to come, we considered the impact on the therapeutic process of unrecognized correspondences and disparities between the patient's and analyst's respective worlds of experience. In psychoanalytic treatment the impact of the observer was grasped as intrinsic to the observed (see also Kohut, 1982, 1984).

In subsequent studies, most conducted in collaboration with Bernard Brandchaft (Stolorow, Brandchaft, and Atwood, 1983, 1987; Atwood and Stolorow, 1984; Brandchaft and Stolorow, 1984; Stolorow and Brandchaft, 1987), we demonstrated that an intersubjective perspective can illuminate a vast array of clinical issues, including negative therapeutic reactions and enactments, therapeutic action and therapeutic alliances, conflict formation and resistance, affective development and pathogenesis, and borderline and psychotic states. We (Stolorow et al., 1987) eventually concluded that "the intersubjective context has a constitutive role in *all* forms of psychopathology" (p. 3) and proposed that "the exploration of the particular patterns of intersubjective transaction involved in developing and maintaining each of the various forms of psychopathology is . . . one of the most important areas for continuing clinical psychoanalytic research" (p. 4).

We wish to emphasize here that our use of the term "intersubjective" has never presupposed the attainment of symbolic thought, of a concept of oneself as subject, or of intersubjective relatedness in Stern's (1985) sense. Although the word "intersubjective" had been used before by developmental psychologists, we were unfamiliar with this prior usage when we (Stolorow et al., 1978) first coined the term independently and assigned it a particular meaning within our evolving framework. Unlike the developmentalists, we use "intersubjective" to refer to *any* psychological field formed by interacting worlds of experience, at whatever developmental level these worlds may be organized.

We also wish to emphasize that, although the development of the theory of intersubjectivity owes much to psychoanalytic self psychology (see Stolorow, 1992), significant differences exist between Kohut's (1971, 1977, 1984) concept of a self-selfobject relationship (a relationship that serves to maintain, restore, or consolidate the organization of self-experience) and our concept of an intersubjective field. An intersubjective field is a system of *reciprocal mutual influence* (Beebe and Lachmann, 1988a). Not only does the patient turn to the analyst for selfobject experiences, but the analyst also turns to the patient for such experiences (Wolf, 1979; Lee, 1988), and a parallel statement can be made about the child-caregiver system as well. To capture this intersubjective reciprocity of mutual influence, one would have to speak of a self-selfobject/selfobject-self relationship.

More importantly, "subjective world" is a construct that covers more experiential territory than "self." Therefore, an intersubjective field—a system formed by the reciprocal interplay between two (or more) subjective worlds—is broader and more inclusive than a self-selfobject relationship. An intersubjective field exists at a higher level of generality and thus can encompass dimensions of experience—such as trauma, conflict, defense, and resistance—other than the selfobject dimension.

The perspective of intersubjectivity is, in its essence, a sweeping methodological and epistemological stance calling for a radical revision of all aspects of psychoanalytic thought. Our earlier work brought into focus the implications of this stance for a broad range of clinical issues and problems that are critical in the practice of psychoanalytic therapy. In the present book we extend the intersubjectivity principle to a rethinking of the foundational pillars of psychoanalytic theory, including the concept of the unconscious, the relation between mind and body, the concept of trauma, and the understanding of fantasy. We begin first with a critique of an idea that has long obstructed the recognition of the intersubjective foundations of psychological life—the concept of an isolated, individual mind. By offering a critical exposition of this idea as it has appeared in various psychoanalytic theories, we hope to bring the assumptions underlying our own viewpoint more clearly into view and to situate our framework within the spectrum of psychoanalytic thought.

I

Theoretical Foundations

Chapter 1

The Myth of the Isolated Mind

IN CONTRAST WITH THE VIEW that modern man suffers from an absence of myth, in this chapter we challenge a central myth that pervades contemporary Western culture and has insinuated itself into the foundational assumptions of psychoanalysis – The Myth of the Isolated Individual Mind. By bringing into focus the unconscious organizing power of this myth and proposing an alternative perspective emphasizing the intersubjective foundations of psychological life, we hope to contribute not only to the advancement of psychoanalytic theory but also to the deepening of reflective self-awareness. Liberated from the constraining grip of this myth, psychoanalytic theorizing will be freed to picture human experience in radically new ways.

ALIENATION AND THE ISOLATED MIND

The myth of the isolated mind ascribes to man a mode of being in which the individual exists separately from the world of physical nature and also from engagement with others. This myth in addition denies the essential immateriality of human experience by portraying subjective life in reified, substantialized terms. Viewed as a symbol of cultural experience, the image of the isolated mind represents modern man's alienation from nature, from social life, and from subjectivity itself. This alienation, still so pervasive in our time, has much to do with the culture of technocracy and the associated intellectual heritage of mechanism that have dominated thought about human nature in the 20th century (Matson, 1964; Barrett, 1979). Our purpose in what follows, however, is not to offer a critique of such cultural and historical factors, but rather to explore the psychological meanings underlying the myth of the isolated mind.

It is our view that modern man's threefold alienation serves to disavow a set of specific vulnerabilities that are inherent in human existence, vulnerabilities that otherwise may lead to an unbearable sense of anxiety and anguish. We shall consider first the embeddedness of human life in the world of physical nature.

Alienation from Nature

Positing the existence of mind as an entity introduces a distinction within man's constitution between bodily and mental forms of being. This distinction diminishes the experience of the inescapable physical embodiment of the human self and thereby attenuates a sense of being wholly subject to the conditions and cycles of biological existence. These conditions include absolute dependence on the physical environment, kinship to other animals, subjection to biological rhythms and needs, and, perhaps most important, man's physical vulnerability and ultimate mortality. Inherent in an unalienated attitude toward mortality – the certainty and finality of biological death – is anxiety at the prospect of physical annihilation and anguish in the face of the transitoriness of all things. Insofar as the being of man is defined and located in mind, existing as an entity apart from the embeddedness of the body in the biological world, an illusion can be maintained that there is a sphere of inner freedom from the constraints of animal existence and mortality. This reassuring differentiation from physical nature may pass over into frank reifications of the self as an immortal essence that literally transcends the cycle of life and death. Such reifications take many forms, including the various concepts of the immortal soul, identifications of the self with ideas and works considered to have everlasting significance and value, and projections of the self into lines of descendants extending indefinitely into the future (Rank, 1930; Becker, 1973, 1975).

We distinguish between the unalienated experience of the physical embodiment of the self just discussed and a class of defensive states entailing wholesale identifications of the self with the physical body. These latter states, corresponding on a psychological level to philosophical doctrines of crude materialism and behaviorism, involve an effort to nullify subjectivity and reduce human existence to the exclusive terms of pure physicality. As the person becomes solely matter or body, there is no experience of anguish in reaction to mortality because experience itself has been denied. Moreover, death loses much of its power in a world that has become entirely material and concrete, because there is then no life of a conscious subject that inevitably becomes obliterated, but rather only the cessation of a particular set of physiological processes.

Alienation from Social Life

A second realm of alienation symbolized in the myth of the isolated mind is that of the individual's relationship to other human beings. The idea of mind as a separate entity implies an independence of the essential being of the person from engagement with others. The image of this mental entity, located in the midst of reality and subsisting alongside other minds, reifies in the first place the widespread experience of psychological aloneness. It is said by those who have fallen under the power of this myth that each individual knows only his own consciousness and is thus forever barred from direct access to experiences belonging to other people. This ostensibly "ontological" aloneness (Mijuscovic, 1988), which ignores the constitutive role of the relationship to the other in a person's having any experience at all, attributes universality to a quite particular subjective state characterized by a sense of imprisoning estrangement from others. This is a state in which one feels neither known nor understood at the level of one's deepest affects; it is, moreover, one in which the longing for such sustaining connection to others has succumbed to resignation and hopelessness. This isolation, so pervasive and deeply rooted in our culture, provides, in our view, the specific intersubjective context that renders the experience of anguish unbearable and necessitates the disavowals of vulnerability inherent in the myth of the isolated mind. The pain associated with modern man's alienated aloneness is, in addition, diminished within this myth by the calming vision of personal isolation being built into the human condition as the common fate of all mankind.

Other experiences reified in the image of the isolated mind include those of psychological distinctness and self-constancy. Inherent in the idea of the mind's existence as an entity is a notion of its separateness from other minds and from a surrounding reality. Separateness is seen as belonging to the mind-entity as an intrinsic feature of its being and is thus not understood to be contingent on any particular relation between the person and the surround. This we contrast with the *experience* of psychological distinctness, a structuralization of self-awareness that is wholly embedded in formative and sustaining intersubjective contexts. Similarly in the case of constancy, the mythical image of mind is one of a quasi-spatial thing that retains an enduring integrity as an absolute property of its nature. The structure of mind as such is regarded as possessing its own internal constancy, even though specific contents of mind may be viewed as changing over time. This idea again strikes a contrast with *experiences* of self-constancy and of the continuity of personal identity, which always derive from constitutive intersubjective contexts.

An unalienated attitude toward man's irreducible engagement with others leads to an experience of anguish at the fate of human beings to be so irrevocably dependent on and vulnerable to events occurring in the interpersonal milieu. The intrinsic embeddedness of self-experience in intersubjective fields means that our self-esteem, our sense of personal identity, even our experience of ourselves as having distinct and enduring existence are contingent on specific sustaining relations to the human surround. The reifications being discussed create reassuring illusions of self-sufficiency and autonomy and thus serve to disavow the intolerable vulnerability of the very structure of psychological life to interpersonal events over which the individual has only limited control.

Alienation from Subjectivity

The third and most important form of alienation is man's estrangement from the features of subjectivity itself. The disavowals of vulnerability crystalized in the myth of the isolated mind, as noted earlier, are achieved through the reification of various dimensions of subjectivity. These reifications confer upon experience one or another of the properties ordinarily attributed to things on the plane of material reality, for example, spatial localization, extension, enduring substantiality, and the like. The mind thus takes its place as a thing among things. Lost in the process are the properties of subjective life itself, which becomes swallowed up inside the reified mind-entity and conceived in terms of categories applying to tangible objects in the physical world.

Invariably associated with the image of mind is that of an external reality or world upon which the mind-entity is presumed to look out. Here too we encounter a reification, in this case one involving the experience of the world as real and existing separately from the self. What psychological purpose can be ascribed to the reifying of the experience that there is an enduring world distinct from the self? Within the myth of the isolated mind, this world is viewed as having a definitive existence of its own; its experienced substantiality thereby becomes transformed into a metaphysical absolute, a universal that is valid for all human beings. This stands in contrast to the *subjective sense* that there is an enduring and substantial world of reality separate from the self, again an experience constituted and sustained by particular intersubjective fields. The vulnerability disavowed by reifying the experience of the world outside the self stems from a certain insecurity deeply rooted in the conditions of modern life. If even the permanence and substantiality of the world are constituted and maintained by intersubjective fields, in a culture of pervasive psychological aloneness there is little to protect a person from feeling that the solidity of things is dissolving into thin air.

The image of the mind looking out on the external world is a heroic image or heroic myth, in that it portrays the inner essence of the person surviving in a state that is separated from all that actually sustains life. This myth appears in many guises and variations. One can discern its presence in tales of invincible persons who overcome great adversity through solitary heroic acts, in philosophical works revolving around a conception of an isolated, monadic subject, and in psychological and psychoanalytic doctrines focusing exclusively on processes occurring within the autonomous person. We turn now to a discussion of the guises of the myth of mind as they appear in classical and contemporary psychoanalysis.

VARIANTS OF THE ISOLATED MIND

In psychoanalysis, the stage was set for the various versions of the doctrine of the isolated mind by its founder, Freud. In virtually all phases of his metapsychological theorizing, Freud pictured the mind as a "mental apparatus," an energy-disposal machine that channels drive energies arising endogenously from within the interior of the organism. In this vision, the developing organization of experience is shaped by the mind's successes, failures, and compromises in the processing of drive energies emerging from within. The experience of one's surround, for example, is shaped by the vicissitudes of innate drive pressures, and the surround contributes to the organization of experience only insofar as it affects those drive vicissitudes. Accordingly, the organization of experience is ultimately the product of internal forces, and the mind's insularity is symbolically reified in the image of an impersonal machine. This image has insinuated itself into all the variants of Freudian psychoanalytic theory.

In Freudian ego psychology, for example, the importance of the surround in the regulation of *early* developmental experiences is acknowledged–what Mitchell (1988) aptly terms the "developmental tilt"–but the image of an isolated, individual mind is retained in the form of an ideal endpoint of optimal development. Hartmann (1939) conceptualized ego development as a process whereby regulation by the environment comes to be replaced by autonomous self-regulation, an evolution that he cast in a reified spatial metaphor by designating it "internalization," as if the surround eventually becomes unnecessary because it is literally "taken in." This idolatry of the autonomous mind finds vivid expression in Jacobson's (1964) description of the experiential consequences of superego formation. Prior to this developmental achievement, according to her view, the child's self-esteem is highly vulnerable to the impact of experiences with others. As a result of the consolidation of the superego, by contrast, self-esteem is said to become stabilized and relatively independent of relations with others, so that it "cannot be as easily affected as before by experiences of rejection, frustration, failure and the like" and is "apt to withstand . . . psychic or even physical injuries to the self" (p. 132). In this model, the vulnerability of self-esteem that derives from the embeddedness of self-experience in a shifting intersubjective context is reserved for early childhood, *prior* to the structuralization of the psyche. The autonomous ego of the healthy older child or adult, by contrast, is presumed to have achieved immunity from the "slings and arrows" encountered in experiences of the surround.

This ego-psychological view of development, emphasizing autonomy as its successful outcome, was preserved in Kohut's (1971) early theory of self-structure formation through "optimal frustration" leading to "transmuting internalization"–the gradual formation of particles of psychic structure that exercise regulatory functions heretofore performed by others. As we develop more fully in the next section and in chapter 4, we would replace the theory of transmuting internalization, which elevates a variant of the isolated mind to an ideal goal of development, with a conception of increasing affect integration and tolerance evolving within an ongoing intersubjective system (Socarides and Stolorow, 1984/85; Stolorow et al., 1987). Emotional experience, we contend, is always regulated and constituted within an intersubjective context.

As an example of the clinical consequences of ego psychology's idealization of autonomy, consider the familiar notion that in the successful termination phase of an analysis the transference should be resolved or dissolved, meaning that the patient's emotional attachment to the analyst must be renounced. In this view, residual transference feelings are seen as an infantilizing element, undermining the patient's progress toward independence. The autonomous, isolated mind is pictured here not only as the endpoint of optimal early development but as the ideal outcome of a successful psychoanalysis.[1] In contrast, a perspective that recognizes that experience and its organization are inextricably embedded in an intersubjective context can accept and even welcome the patient's remaining tie to the analyst as a potential source of emotional sustenance for the future (Stolorow and Lachmann, 1984/85; Stolorow et al., 1987).

Remnants of the doctrine of the isolated mind can also be found in a number of theoretical frameworks that have been posed as radical alternatives to Freudian ego psychology—for example, Schafer's action language, object relations theory, Kohut's self psychology, and interpersonal psychoanalysis.

Schafer (1976) has argued cogently that the structural-energic constructs of Freudian ego psychology represent unlabeled spatial metaphors, concretistic reifications of nonsubstantial subjective experiences such as fantasies. Metapsychological concepts such as psychic structures, forces, and energies treat subjective states as though they were thinglike entities possessing such properties as substance, quantity, extension, momentum, and location. Schafer proposes a new "action language" for psychoanalysis. This would do away with mechanistic metapsychological reifications and would focus on the person-as-agent—that is, on the person as a performer of actions who, consciously and unconsciously, authors his own life. Within this framework, the subject matter of psychoanalytic conceptualization and interpretation becomes action itself, especially disclaimed action, along with the person's conscious and unconscious personal reasons for his actions.

While we have found Schafer's critique of Freudian metapsychology to be exceedingly valuable, it seems to us that he is no less guilty of reifying an aspect of experience than those whom

---

[1]We are grateful to Dr. Sheila Namir for calling this point to our attention.

he criticizes. The dimension that Schafer substantializes and universalizes is the *experience of personal agency*. Indeed, in Schafer's system the experience of agency is elevated to the ontological core of psychological life. Hence, his framework cannot encompass those experiential states in which the sense of personal agency has remained atrophied or precarious in consequence of developmental interferences and derailments. More important, the continual embeddedness of the sense of agency, and of self-experience in general, in a nexus of intersubjective relatedness becomes, in Schafer's vision, obscured by the reified image of an omnipotent agent single-handedly creating his own experiences—another variant of the isolated mind in action.

The omnipotence of the individual mind reaches its pinnacle in certain versions of Kleinian object relations theory, most notably in the clinical application of the concept of projective identification. Kernberg (1975), for example, transforms Klein's (1950) description of a primitive fantasy into a causally efficacious mechanism through which a person is presumed to translocate parts of himself into the psyche and soma of another. Consider, in this regard, his discussion of Ingmar Bergman's movie, *Persona*:

> A recent motion picture . . . illustrates the breakdown of an immature but basically decent young woman, a nurse, charged with the care of a psychologically severely ill woman presenting . . . a typical narcissistic personality. In the face of the cold, unscrupulous exploitation to which the young nurse is subjected, she gradually breaks down. . . . The sick woman seems to be able to live only if and when she can destroy what is valuable in other persons. . . . In a dramatic development, the nurse develops an intense hatred for the sick woman and mistreats her cruelly at one point. *It is as if all the hatred within the sick woman had been transferred into the helping one, destroying the helping person from the inside* [pp. 245–246, emphasis added].

Here we see a caricature of the isolated mind unleashed. The subject is viewed as creating not only her own experiences, but even the other's experiences as well. A unidirectional influence system is pictured, wherein everything that one experiences from the surround is seen as being the product of one's own omnipotent intrapsychic activity. The impact of the surround is nowhere to be found.

Kernberg (1976) has offered a revision of Freudian drive theory in which he pictures the basic building blocks of personality structure as units consisting of a self-image, an object (other) image, and an affect. Units with a positive affective valence are said to coalesce into the libidinal drive, while those with a negative valence form the basis for the aggressive drive. Although Kernberg acknowledges the developmental and motivational importance of affect, once integrated into enduring self-object-affect units, affect states are seen to behave like drives, stirring within the confines of an isolated mind and triggering all manner of distorting defensive activity. The life-long embeddedness of affective experience in an ongoing intersubjective system thereby becomes lost.

Kohut's self psychology has made enormous strides toward loosening the grip of the doctrine of the isolated mind on contemporary psychoanalytic thought. The concept of "selfobject function" (Kohut, 1971, 1977, 1984), in emphasizing that the organization of self-experience is always codetermined by the felt responsiveness of others, is a prime example. In striking contrast to the ego-psychological view of development, Kohut (1984) wrote:

> Self psychology holds that self-selfobject relationships form the essence of psychological life from birth to death, that a move from dependence (symbiosis) to independence (autonomy) in the psychological sphere is no more possible . . . than a corresponding move from a life dependent on oxygen to a life independent of it in the biological sphere [p. 47].

In regard to the psychoanalytic situation, one of the most important contributions of self psychology has been the heightened attention to the impact of the analyst/investigator on the field that he investigates. Kohut (1984) drew a parallel between the shift from traditional analysis to self psychology and the shift from Newtonian physics to the Planckian physics of atomic and subatomic particles, in which "the field that is observed, of necessity, includes the observer" (p. 41). Whereas, according to Kohut, traditional analysis "sees the analyst only as the observer and the analysand only as the field that the observer-analyst surveys," the self-psychological orientation "acknowledges and then examines the analyst's influence . . . as an intrinsically significant human presence" (p. 37).

Despite such powerful challenges to the myth of the isolated mind, relics of this myth still persist in self-psychological writings. One such remnant can be found in the persistent use of the term *self* to refer both to an existential agent (an independent initiator of action, Schafer's focus) and a psychological structure (the organization of self-experience). As we have discussed in another context (Stolorow et al., 1987), some of the theoretical difficulties that result from the conflation of these two usages can be illustrated by the following sentence, typical of many that appear in the literature of self psychology: "The fragmented self strives to restore its cohesion." Here the term self has two distinctly different referents: (1) an organization of experience (called the self) has undergone fragmentation, and (2) an existential agent (also called the self) is performing actions to restore cohesion to that organization of experience. This creates a theoretical conundrum. Clearly, it is not the pieces of something (fragments of a self) that strive toward a goal (restoration). More important, the second usage of self as an independent existential entity transforms the experiential, agentic "I" into a reified "it," not unlike the impersonal mental apparatus of Freudian theory. This residue of the doctrine of the isolated mind clouds Kohut's central contribution – the recognition that *self-experience* is always organized within a constitutive intersubjective context.

A second remnant of the myth of the isolated mind that persists in self psychology can be seen in the idea that the self possesses an innate nuclear program or inherent design (Kohut, 1984) awaiting a responsive milieu that will enable it to unfold (see Mitchell, 1988). Unlike ego psychology, which postulates the autonomous mind as the ideal endpoint of development, self psychology seems here to locate this ideal in the prenatal or genetic prehistory of the individual, as a preexisting potential requiring only the opportunity to become actualized. Such an idea contrasts sharply with our view that the trajectory of self-experience is shaped at every point in development by the intersubjective system in which it crystalizes.

As Bacal and Newman (1990) have pointed out, Kohut seemed reluctant to consider his framework a relational theory, probably because he wanted to preserve its link to the intrapsychic tradition of Freudian psychoanalysis. Yet the pervasive reifications of the concepts of the self, the selfobject, and the self-selfobject relationship threaten to transform self psychology into just the sort of crude interpersonalism or social interactionism that Kohut wished to eschew. A solution to this quandary can be found in the perspective of intersubjectivity. The concept of an intersubjective system brings to focus *both* the individual's world of inner experience *and* its embeddedness with other such worlds in a continual flow of reciprocal mutual influence. In this vision, the gap between the intrapsychic and interpersonal realms is closed, and, indeed, the old dichotomy between them is rendered obsolete (see also Beebe, Jaffe, and Lachmann, 1992).

Another variation on the theme of the isolated mind is found in the recent theoretical formulations of Basch (1988). Basch's work is particularly interesting to consider because he is both a prominent advocate of Kohut's self psychology and an outspoken representative of a trend in contemporary psychoanalysis that seeks to ground psychoanalytic theory in the neurosciences. He presents a conceptual framework intended to bridge the "longstanding and counterproductive gap between psychology and biology," a "scientifically based . . . unified, and unifying theory of psychotherapy" (p. 15). The unification of psychology and biology is here attempted in a way that returns to the spirit of Freud's (1895) ill-fated "Project for a Scientific Psychology," namely, the reduction of psychological functioning to mechanistic processes occurring within the human nervous system. Basch, relying on metaphorical imagery drawn from modern cybernetics and computer science, envisions psychological activity as essentially pattern-matching, error-correcting feedback cycles taking place inside the brain.

There are two major aspects of Basch's (1988) thinking that betray the infiltration of his writings by the myth of the isolated mind. The first of these concerns his view of the relationship between the person and reality. He argues that the individual stands in relation, not to an external world having an independent existence of its own, but always and only to a reality that "is a construction created by the brain of the beholder" (p. 60). For example, he suggests that when he once went in search of a lost piece of soap, although he may have felt that he was looking for something located in a world outside of himself, actually he was trying to find "a pattern of sensory signals that would add up to what [he] already had inside his head–an encoded pattern of sensory features labeled 'soap' " (p. 60). Even one's mother and father are seen as not possessing any literal existence in a world apart from the self but are regarded instead as examples of "imaginary entities that exist only in the brain" (p. 101). Presumably when one searches for a missing parent, as in the case of the lost soap, one is actually trying to find perceptual and affective signals that add up to what is located only in one's head: the assembly of characteristics labeled "mother" or "father." Here we see a position of radical constructivism verging on solipsism, and one moreover that situates itself inside the physical boundaries of the human cranium. This position appears to involve a self-contradiction: it contains on one level a claim that at another level it denies. On one hand, Basch denies the literal truth of the individual's experience of the independent existence of objects outside the boundaries of the self; he argues that such objects are only "constructions" localized inside the human brain. On the other hand, Basch does accord independent existence to one class of such external objects; the brains themselves. This seeming paradox arises, in our view, from Basch's unacknowledged use of the brain as a reified symbol of the isolated mind, which produces experiences out of its own autonomous constructive activity.

The second way in which the myth of the isolated mind becomes manifest in Basch's conceptualizations appears in his views of human motivation and especially the sources of individual self-esteem. According to Basch, the prime motivator underlying all psychological activity is the quest for *competence,* which he defines as "the brain's capacity to establish order among the disparate stimuli that continuously bombard the senses" (p. 27). On the level of introspection and reflection,

competence becomes the experience of self-esteem. Basch elabo-
rates: "True self-esteem, a genuine sense of one's self as worthy
of nurture and protection . . . stems from the experience of
competence, the experience of functioning appropriately . . . *no
one can give another the experience of competence: one must achieve that
for oneself"* (p. 26, emphasis added).

He further clarifies: "the standard by which one judges one's
own competence or incompetence is always internal, not external" (p. 59). This judgment of competence and self-esteem is
made in terms of matches or mismatches between brain representations of one's behavior or circumstances and preexisting
neural patterns functioning as the goal that is being pursued.
This curious doctrine specifically denies that experiences of
competence and self-esteem derive from interpersonal transactions pertaining to one's sense of oneself in the human community. Again we encounter the autonomous subject who needs
little more than internal arrays of sensory signals matching with
previously encoded neurological patterns in order to be sustained
and to function as a human being.

Consider now the central construct in Basch's metapsychology, the so-called *self-system.* This system is defined as a biological entity consisting of a hierarchical organization of interrelated, error-correcting feedback cycles. Although Basch states
that it is unsatisfactory to reduce the complex activity usually
denoted by the term mind to the neurological activity of the
brain, his concept of the self-system does precisely that. This
entity is a creation of the brain, is located within the brain, and
controls and guides the brain in its relation to the world. The
self-system moreover is pictured as enabling the brain to function "as a self-programming computer" (p. 106) using arrange-
ments of "software" that function as "the guardians of order, the
ensurers of competence and, ultimately, of self-esteem" (p. 105).
In this image of the brain as a self-programming computer
relating only to its own internal constructions, we find a dramatic materialization of the isolated mind within a physiological organ that has been endowed with the attributes of person-
hood.

Interpersonal psychoanalysis grew out of Sullivan's (1953)
attempt to replace the intrapsychic determinism of Freudian

theory with an emphasis on the centrality of social interaction. Indeed, Sullivan wished to resituate psychiatry and psychoanalysis within the domain of the social sciences. His efforts were marred, in our view, by the vacillation of his investigatory stance from one that assumed a position *within* the experiential worlds of those involved in an interaction (an intersubjective perspective) to one that stood *outside* the transaction and presumed to make objective observations that were subject to "consensual validation." The latter stance is illustrated by Sullivan's concept of "parataxic distortion," a process through which a person's current experiences of others are said to be "warped" in consequence of his past interpersonal history. We wish to emphasize here that the concept of parataxic distortion enshrines another variant of the doctrine of the isolated mind, a mind separated from an "objective" reality that it either accurately apprehends or distorts. This objectivist stance contrasts with an intersubjective one, in which it is assumed that one's personal reality is *always* codetermined by features of the surround and the unique meanings into which these are assimilated.

Contemporary interpersonal psychoanalysis is well represented by Mitchell's (1988) effort to develop an integrated "relational model," drawing on the work of Sullivan and British object relations theorists, most notably, Fairbairn (1952). Mitchell's general description of relational-model theorizing in psychoanalysis is highly compatible with our own viewpoint:

> In this vision the basic unit of study is not the individual as a separate entity whose desires clash with an external reality, but an interactional field within which the individual arises and struggles to make contact and to articulate himself. *Desire* is experienced always *in the context of relatedness,* and it is that context which defines its meaning. Mind is composed of relational configurations. . . . Experience is understood as structured through interactions . . . [pp. 3–4].

Despite the harmony that exists between his overall vision and an intersubjective perspective, remnants of the isolated mind appear in Mitchell's work, particularly in the clinical application of his ideas to the psychoanalytic situation. He describes the analytic patient as continually engaging in "gambits" de-signed to draw the analyst into old relational patterns to which the patient has remained committed and deeply loyal. The ana-lyst, in turn, is said inevitably to find himself a "coactor" in the patient's passionate drama, "enacting the *patient's* old scenarios" (p. 293) and inexorably falling into "the patient's predesigned categories" (p. 295). The patient–or better, the patient's mind–is pictured here as the chief director of the analytic stage, much in the manner of Schafer's (1976) omnipotent agent and the unidirectional influence system embodied in the theory of pro-jective identification. Insufficient attention is given to the pa-tient's becoming a coactor in the *analyst's* drama, to the recip-rocal impact on the patient's experience of the *analyst's* predesigned categories (including the assumption that patients engage in gambits), as conveyed, for example, by the analyst's interpretations. In his clinical approach, it seems to us, Mit-chell's elegant relational model ultimately collapses into a variant of the myth of the individual mind.

Why is it that the isolated mind, as we have seen, is such a difficult demon to exorcise, even for those who have so assidu-ously devoted themselves to the task? As we proposed earlier, it is our view that this pervasive, reified image in its many guises serves to disavow the exquisite vulnerability that is inherent to an unalienated awareness of the continual embeddedness of human experience in a constitutive intersubjective context. The impersonal machine, the autonomous ego, the omnipotent agent, the inviolable pristine self–all such images of the mind insulated from the constitutive impact of the surround counter-act, to paraphrase Kundera (1984), what might be termed "the unbearable embeddedness of being." Analogously to isolated states in early development (Ogden, 1991), they provide a "buffer against the continual strain of being alive in the world of human beings" (p. 388).

THE ONTOGENY OF PERSONAL EXPERIENCE

We contend that the development of personal experience al-ways takes place within an ongoing intersubjective system.

Earlier, in a chapter written in collaboration with Brandchaft, we (Atwood and Stolorow, 1984) summarized the intersubjective perspective on psychological development:

> [B]oth psychological development and pathogenesis are . . . conceptualized in terms of the specific intersubjective contexts that shape the developmental process and that facilitate or obstruct the child's negotiation of critical developmental tasks and successful passage through developmental phases. The observational focus is the evolving psychological field constituted by the interplay between the differently organized subjectivities of child and caretakers [p. 65].

An impressive body of research evidence has been amassed documenting that the developing organization of the child's experience must be seen as a property of the *child–caregiver system of mutual regulation* (see Lichtenberg, 1983, 1989; Sander, 1985, 1987; Stern, 1985, 1988; Beebe and Lachmann, 1988a,b; Emde, 1988a,b). According to Sander (1985, 1987), it is the infant–caregiver system that regulates and organizes the infant's experience of inner states. The development of self-regulatory competence, therefore, is a *systems competence*. In a more recent work, Sander (1991) has shown that even the sense of distinctness, uniqueness, and personal agency emerges and is sustained within a developmental system in which there is a synchronous "specificity of fittedness" between the infant's shifting states and the caregiver's ability to recognize them. Stern (1985), too, has described in great detail the formation of various senses of self from the child's interactions with "self-regulating others." Beebe and Lachmann (1988a,b) have shown that recurrent patterns of mutual influence between mother and infant provide the basis for the development of self- and object representations. They argue that in the earliest representations what is represented is "an emergent dyadic phenomenon, structures of the interaction, which cannot be described on the basis of either partner alone" (Beebe and Lachmann, 1988a, p. 305). A similar view of the interactional basis of psychic structure formation is implicit in Lichtenberg's (1989) discussion of the schemas or "scripts" that underlie the experience of various motivational

systems and in Emde's (1988a) description of personality structures developing from the internalization of "infant–caregiver
relationship patterns." Each of these authors, in different language, is describing how recurring patterns of intersubjective
transaction within the developmental system result in the establishment of invariant principles that unconsciously organize the
child's subsequent experiences (Atwood and Stolorow, 1984;
Stolorow et al., 1987), a realm of unconsciousness that we term
the "prereflective unconscious" (see chapter 2). It is these unconscious ordering principles, crystalized within the matrix of the
child–caregiver system, that form the essential building blocks
of personality development.

Some may see a contradiction between the concept of developmentally preestablished principles that organize subsequent
experiences and our repeated contention that experience is always embedded in a constitutive intersubjective context. This
contradiction is more apparent than real. A person enters any
situation with an established set of ordering principles (the subject's contribution to the intersubjective system), but it is the
context that determines which among the array of these principles will be called on to organize the experience. Experience
becomes organized by a particular invariant principle only when
there is a situation that lends itself to being so organized. The
organization of experience can therefore be seen as codetermined *both* by preexisting principles *and* by an ongoing context
that favors one or another of them over the others.

Examples of this codetermination are readily seen during the
course of psychoanalytic treatment, in the shifting figure-ground
relationships between what we (Stolorow et al., 1987) have
termed the "selfobject" and "repetitive" dimensions of the transference. In the former, the patient yearns for the analyst to
provide selfobject experiences that were missing or insufficient
during the formative years (Kohut, 1971, 1977, 1984). In the
latter, which is a source of conflict and resistance, the patient
expects and fears a repetition with the analyst of early experiences of developmental failure (Ornstein, 1974). These two
dimensions continually oscillate between the experiential foreground and background of the transference in concert with
perceptions of the analyst's varying attunement to the patient's

emotional states and needs. For example, when the analyst is experienced as malattuned, foreshadowing a traumatic repetition of early developmental failure, the conflictual and resistive dimension is brought into the foreground, and the patient's selfobject longings are driven into hiding. On the other hand, when the analyst is able to analyze accurately the patient's experience of rupture of the therapeutic bond and demonstrate his understanding of the patient's reactive affect states and the principles that organize them, the selfobject dimension becomes restored and strengthened and the conflictual/resistive/repetitive dimension tends to recede into the background.

In our experience, intractable repetitive transferences are codetermined (in varying degrees) *both* by the relentless grip of the patient's invariant principles, a product of the absence or precariousness of alternative principles for organizing experience, *and* by aspects of the analyst's stance that lend themselves to repeated retraumatization of the patient (see chapter 7). Successful psychoanalytic treatment, in our view, does not produce therapeutic change by altering or eliminating the patient's invariant organizing principles. Rather, through new relational experiences with the analyst in concert with enhancements of the patient's capacity for reflective self-awareness, it facilitates the establishment and consolidation of alternative principles and thereby enlarges the patient's experiential repertoire. More generally, it is the formation of new organizing principles within an intersubjective system that constitutes the essence of developmental change throughout the life cycle.

It should be clear that the intersubjective view of psychological development is not to be confused with a naive environmentalism. Rather, it embraces what Wallace (1985) felicitously terms "intersectional causation." At any moment the child's formative experiences are understood to emerge from the intersection of, and to be codetermined by, his psychological organization as it has evolved to that point and specific features of the caregiving surround. In this model, the development of the child's psychological organization is always seen as an aspect of an evolving and maturing child–caregiver system.

Studies of the vicissitudes of the developmental system are giving rise to a radically altered psychoanalytic theory of motivation. Clearly, it is no longer satisfactory to view motivation in terms of the workings of a mental apparatus processing instinctual drive energies. Instead, it has increasingly come to be recognized, as Lichtenberg (1989) aptly argues, that "motivations arise solely from *lived experience*" and that "the vitality of the motivational experience will depend . . . on the manner in which affect-laden exchanges unfold between infants and their caregivers" (p. 2). Most important, in our view, has been the shift from drive to affect as the central motivational construct for psychoanalysis (see Basch, 1984; Demos and Kaplan, 1986; Jones, in press). Affectivity, we now know, is not a product of isolated intrapsychic mechanisms; it is a property of the child–caregiver system of mutual regulation (Sander, 1985; Rogawski, 1987; Demos, 1988). Stern (1985) has described in exquisite detail the regulation of affective experience within the infant–caregiver dyad through processes of intersubjective sharing and mutual affect attunement. The "affective core of the self" (Emde, 1988a) derives from the person's history of intersubjective transactions, and thus the shift from drive to affect resituates the psychoanalytic theory of motivation squarely within the realm of the intersubjective. Early developmental trauma, from this perspective, is viewed not as an instinctual flooding of an ill-equipped mental apparatus. Rather, as we develop in chapter 4, the tendency for affective experiences to create a disorganized or disintegrated self-state is seen to originate from early faulty affect attunements–breakdowns of the infant-caregiver system–leading to the loss of affect-regulatory capacity (Socarides and Stolorow, 1984/85). These are the rock-bottom dangers for which later states of anxiety sound the alarm. As we demonstrate in chapter 2, the shift from drive to affect leads inevitably to an intersubjective view of the formation of psychic conflict and of what has been traditionally termed the "dynamic unconscious."

Let us now consider, from an intersubjective perspective, the development of a constituent of personal experience that has great clinical import–the sense of the real.

The Genesis of the Sense of the Real

We are concerned here with the process by which a child acquires an experience of the world and the self as real. "Reality," as we use the term, refers to something subjective, something felt or sensed, rather than to an external realm of being existing independently of the human subject. In classical Freudian theory, reality is pictured in the latter way, and psychological development is conceptualized as a gradual coming into contact with the constraints and conditions of this independent, external world. Central to the process of establishing contact with reality, according to Freud (1923) and other classical theorists (Ferenczi, 1913; Fenichel, 1945), are experiences of frustration and disappointment. Such inevitable but painful moments supposedly propel the child out of an undifferentiated mode of functioning by contributing to the separation of an ego that takes into account the independence of the external world and operates under the so-called reality principle. Our focus, by contrast, is on the child's establishing a *sense* that what he experiences is real, and on how this sense of the real develops within a facilitating intersubjective matrix.

We have previously highlighted (Stolorow, Atwood, and Brandchaft, 1992) the developmental importance of a selfobject function contributing to the articulation and validation of a child's unfolding world of personal experience, and we have designated this *the self-delineating selfobject function.* It is our view that the development of a child's sense of the real occurs not primarily as a result of frustration and disappointment, but rather through the validating attunement of the caregiving surround, an attunement provided across a whole spectrum of affectively intense, positive and negative experiences. Reality thus crystalizes at the interface of interacting, affectively attuned subjectivities.

The self-delineating selfobject function may be pictured along a developmental continuum, from early sensorimotor forms of validation occurring in the preverbal transactions between infant and caregiver, to later processes of validation that take place increasingly through symbolic communication and involve the child's awareness of others as separate centers of subjectivity.

Preverbal forms of validation are implicit in the sensorimotor dialogue in which the caregiver's sense of the infant's shifting subjective states is expressed. Such communication, occurring primarily through modulations of touch, holding, facial expression, and vocal rhythm and intonation (Stern, 1985), creates an intersubjective field echoing and mirroring the infant's ongoing experiences. This field provides sensorimotor patterns that articulate the different aspects of what the infant perceives and feels, and lays the foundation of the sense of the reality of the world and also of the infant's own nascent self.

New forms of validation become possible once the child becomes aware of others as experiencing subjects (Stern, 1985). In this phase, the caregiver's acts of participatory identification with the child's subjective states increasingly become communicated through verbal and other symbols, permitting the gradual evolution of a symbolic world of self and other experienced by the child as real.

Derailments of this developmental process can occur in any phase when validating attunement is profoundly absent. Under these circumstances, the child, in order to maintain ties vital to well-being, must accommodate the organization of his experience to the caregiver's. With the advent of symbolic communication and awareness of others as centers of subjectivity, such accommodation can result in a subjective world constituted in large part by an alien reality imposed from outside (see Brandchaft, 1991).

Several pathological outcomes of the derailment of the sense of the real are discussed in subsequent chapters: severe narrowing of the domain of reflective self-awareness (chapter 2); disturbances in the development of affectivity and mind-body cohesion (chapter 3); tormenting doubts about the reality of early traumatic injuries and about the validity of one's experience in general (chapters 4 and 5); and the elaboration of dramatic fantasy formations concretizing the process of psychological usurpation (chapter 5).

Chapter 2

Three Realms of the Unconscious

IN THIS CHAPTER WE EXTEND our intersubjective framework to a reconsideration of a cornerstone of all psychoanalytic thought – the concept of unconscious mental processes.

In an earlier attempt to reconceptualize the unconscious, we (Atwood and Stolorow, 1984) distinguished two forms of unconsciousness that are important for psychoanalysis – the prereflective unconscious and the more familiar dynamic unconscious. Both differ from Freud's (1900, 1915) "preconscious" in that they can be made conscious only with great effort. The term prereflective unconscious refers to the shaping of experience by organizing principles that operate outside a person's conscious awareness:

> The organizing principles of a person's subjective world, whether operating positively (giving rise to certain configurations in awareness) or negatively (preventing certain configurations from arising), are themselves unconscious. A person's experiences are shaped by his psychological structures without this shaping becoming the focus of awareness and reflection. We have therefore characterized the structure of a subjective world as *prereflectively unconscious*. This form of unconsciousness is not the product of defensive activity, even though great effort is required to overcome it. In fact, the defenses themselves, when operating

outside a person's awareness, can be seen as merely a special instance of structuring activity that is prereflectively unconscious [Atwood and Stolorow, 1984, p. 36].

In our view of psychological development, we pictured these prereflective structures of experience as crystalizing within the evolving interplay between the subjective worlds of child and caregivers. Prime examples are those organizing principles, traditionally covered by the term *superego,* that derive from the child's perceptions of what is required of him to maintain ties that are vital to his well-being.

In reconsidering the dynamic unconscious, we first attempted to formulate its essence in experience-near terms, stripped of metapsychological encumbrances:

[R]epression is understood as a process whereby particular configurations of self and object are prevented from crystalizing in awareness. . . . The "dynamic unconscious," from this point of view, consists in that set of configurations that consciousness is not permitted to assume, because of their association with emotional conflict and subjective danger. Particular memories, fantasies, feelings, and other experiential contents are repressed because they threaten to actualize these configurations [Atwood and Stolorow, 1984, p. 35].

Later we (Stolorow et al., 1987) proposed that the psychological phenomena traditionally encompassed by the concept of the dynamic unconscious derive specifically from the realm of intersubjective transaction that Stern (1985) refers to as "interaffectivity"—the mutual regulation of affective experience within the developmental system. We wrote:

The specific intersubjective contexts in which conflict takes form are those in which central affect states of the child cannot be integrated because they fail to evoke the requisite attuned responsiveness from the caregiving surround. Such unintegrated affect states become the source of lifelong inner conflict, because they are experienced as threats both to the person's established psychological organization and to the maintenance of vitally needed ties. Thus affect-dissociating defensive operations are called into play, which reappear in the analytic situation in the form of resistance. . . . It is in the defensive walling off of central affect states, rooted in early derailments of affect integration, that the origins of what has traditionally been called the "dynamic unconscious" can be found [pp. 91–92].

From this perspective, the dynamic unconscious is seen to consist not of repressed instinctual drive derivatives, but of affect states that have been defensively walled off because they failed to evoke attuned responsiveness from the early surround. This defensive sequestering of central affective states, which attempts to protect against retraumatization, is the principal source of resistance in psychoanalytic treatment, and also of the necessity for disguise when such states are represented in dreams (Stolorow, 1989).

The shift from drives to affectivity as forming the basis for the dynamic unconscious is not merely a change in terminology. As we discussed in chapter 1, the regulation of affective experience is a property of the child–caregiver system of reciprocal mutual influence. If we understand the dynamic unconscious as taking form within such a system, then it becomes apparent that the boundary between conscious and unconscious is always the product of a specific intersubjective context.

With its focus on the vicissitudes of unconscious mental processes, psychoanalysis has, until quite recently, had little to say about the ontogeny of consciousness. It is our view, as we stated in chapter 1, that the child's conscious experience becomes progressively *articulated* through the validating responsiveness of the early surround. The child's affective experience, for example, becomes increasingly differentiated and cognitively elaborated through the attuned responsiveness of caregivers to his emotional states and needs (Socarides and Stolorow, 1984/85). Such attunement must, of course, be communicated in a form that coincides with the child's unfolding psychological capacities.

It follows from this conception of consciousness becoming articulated within an intersubjective system that two closely interrelated forms of unconsciousness may develop from situations in which the requisite validating responsiveness is absent.[1] When a child's experiences are consistently not responded to or are actively rejected, the child perceives that aspects of his own experience are unwelcome or damaging to the caregiver. Whole sectors of the child's experiential world must then be sacrificed (repressed) in order to safeguard the needed tie. This, we have suggested, is the origin of the dynamic unconscious. In addition, other features of the child's experience may remain unconscious, not because they have been repressed, but because, in the absence of a validating intersubjective context, they simply never were able to become articulated. In both instances, the boundary between conscious and unconscious is revealed to be a fluid and ever-shifting one, a product of the changing responsiveness of the surround to different regions of the child's experience. We believe that this conceptualization continues to apply beyond the period of childhood and is readily demonstrated in the psychoanalytic situation as well, wherein the patient's resistance can be seen to fluctuate in concert with perceptions of the analyst's varying receptivity and attunement to the patient's experience. The idea of a fluid boundary forming within an intersubjective system contrasts sharply with the traditional notion of the repression barrier as a fixed intrapsychic structure, "a sharp and final division" (Freud, 1915, p. 195) separating conscious and unconscious contents.

During the preverbal period of infancy, the articulation of the child's experience is achieved through attunements communicated in the sensorimotor dialogue with caregivers (Stern, 1985). During this earliest phase, unconsciousness results from situations of unattunement or misattunement. By the middle of the second year, the child is able to use symbols, making language possible. This is a momentous step in the development of consciousness because henceforth the child's experience increasingly becomes articulated by being encoded in verbal symbols. As Stern (1985) emphasizes, symbols make possible "a sharing of mutually created meanings about personal experience" (p. 172).

---

[1]In an earlier work (Stolorow et al., 1987), we suggested that massive developmental failure in the function of validation of perception is an important factor in the predisposition to psychotic states.

With the maturation of the child's symbolic capacities, symbols gradually assume a place of importance alongside sensorimotor attunements as vehicles through which the child's experience is validated within the developmental system. In that realm of experience in which consciousness increasingly becomes articulated in symbols, unconscious becomes coextensive with unsymbolized. When the act of articulating an experience is perceived to threaten an indispensable tie, repression can now be achieved by preventing the continuation of the process of encoding that experience in symbols. At this point in the development of consciousness, aspects of Freud's (1915) formulation of the process of repression can be seen to apply: "A presentation which is not put into words . . . remains thereafter in the *Ucs.* in a state of repression" (p. 202).

To summarize, we can distinguish three interrelated forms of unconsciousness: (1) the *prereflective unconscious*–the organizing principles that unconsciously shape and thematize a person's experiences; (2) *the dynamic unconscious*–experiences that were denied articulation because they were perceived to threaten needed ties; and (3) the *unvalidated unconscious*–experiences that could not be articulated because they never evoked the requisite validating responsiveness from the surround. All three forms of unconsciousness, we have emphasized, derive from specific, formative intersubjective contexts.

We believe that this experience-near conceptualization of the unconscious, its different realms and their origins, provides a definitive answer to those critics (e.g., Kernberg, 1982) who claim that an empathic-introspective psychology of the subjective world can only remain a psychology of the conscious, and also to those theorists (e.g., Rubinstein, 1976) who argue that the existence of unconscious mental processes can be explained only by resorting to experience-distant concepts borrowed from neurobiology. We define the stance of sustained empathic inquiry as a method for investigating the principles *unconsciously* organizing experience. By emphasizing the analyst's *investigative* activity, this definition supplies an antidote to those counter-transference-based misconstruals of analytic empathy that amalgamate it with a requirement literally and concretely to fulfill a patient's selfobject longings and archaic hopes.

It is our view that the mode of therapeutic action of psychoanalytic treatment differs in each of the three realms of unconsciousness that we have described. Psychoanalysis is, above all
else, a method for illuminating the prereflective unconscious,
and it achieves this aim by investigating the ways in which the
patient's experience of the analytic relationship is unconsciously
and recurrently patterned by the patient according to developmentally preformed meanings and invariant themes. Such analysis, from a position within the patient's subjective frame of
reference, with the codetermining impact of the analyst on the
organization of the patient's experience always kept in view,
both facilitates the engagement and expansion of the patient's
capacity for self-reflection and gradually establishes the analyst
as an understanding presence to whom the patient's formerly
invariant ordering principles must accommodate, inviting syn-
theses of alternative modes of experiencing self and other.

The dynamic unconscious becomes transformed primarily
through analysis of resistance – that is, the investigation of the
patient's expectations and fears in the transference that if his
central affective states and developmental longings are exposed
to the analyst, they will meet with the same traumatogenic,
faulty responsiveness that they received from the original caregivers. Such analysis, always taking into account what the patient
has perceived of the analyst that has lent itself to the patient's
anticipations of retraumatization, establishes the analytic bond
as a gradually expanding zone of safety within which previously sequestered regions of the patient's experience can be
brought out of hiding and integrated.

Analytic attention to the realm of the unvalidated unconscious probably makes a contribution to all analyses, but is
especially important in the treatment of patients who have
suffered severe developmental derailments in the articulation of
perceptual and affective experience. These are patients, often
prone to fragmented, disorganized, or psychosomatic states, for
whom broad areas of early experience failed to evoke validating
attunement from caregivers and, consequently, whose perceptions remain ill-defined and precariously held, easily usurped by
the judgments of others, and whose affects tend to be felt as
diffuse bodily states rather than as symbolically elaborated feel-

ings. In such cases, the analyst's investigation of and attunement to the patient's inner experiences, always from within the patient's perspective, serves to articulate and consolidate the patient's subjective reality, crystalizing the patient's experience, lifting it to higher levels of organization, and strengthening the patient's confidence in its validity. This, we contend, is a foundation stone of the sense of self, a selfobject function so vital and basic that we designate its appearance in analysis by a specific term – the *self-delineating selfobject transference* (Stolorow et al., 1992).

Let us turn now to a visual analogy that we have found useful in discussions of these ideas with students and colleagues. Our purpose here is not to introduce a new topographic model of the mind, complete with reified spatial metaphors, but rather to highlight certain interrelationships between the three forms of unconsciousness once they have become established in the course of development. Imagine a building with several floors and a basement that lies below the surface of the ground. Consciousness corresponds here to the parts of the building above ground level; the higher floors represent those areas of awareness in which a person has achieved comparatively greater development and integration. The dynamic unconscious appears in the basement of the structure below ground and out of sight. Here lie the contents that are driven out of conscious awareness, because of their association with intolerable conflict and subjective danger. The prereflective unconscious has no concrete counterpart in this image, but, rather, corresponds to an architect's blueprint, which sets out the plan according to which a building is constructed. A blueprint may be thought of as a set of organizing principles that specify a pattern of relationships between the various parts of the building. Prereflective structures of experience likewise are not specific subjective contents, but are the principles that organize those contents into characteristic patterns. The unvalidated unconscious appears in our analogy in the form of bricks, lumber, and other unused materials left lying around the building and in the basement, materials that were never made part of the construction but that could have been. These various objects represent experiences that have never been articulated and integrated into the structure of consciousness and that in consequence remain largely unconscious as long as the requisite validation continues to be absent.

CLINICAL ILLUSTRATION

In what follows, we illustrate, through a discussion of a dream, the different forms of unconsciousness. The dream we have selected is a very brief one that occurred at the onset of a psychotic episode experienced by a 19-year-old woman.

> The dreamer stood in a country setting before a small structure that she said resembled an outhouse. Looking inside, she found a toilet. As she peered into the bowl, the water began gurgling, foaming, and then rising and overflowing. The flow became more and more agitated until an explosive geyser of unidentified glowing material erupted from the toilet, increasing in violence without apparent limit. At this point the dreamer awoke in terror.

The nuclear formative situation of this patient's childhood history involved severe sexual exploitation by her father. Commencing at the age of two, her father had used his daughter for primarily oral sexual gratification several times each week. These practices, carried out late at night, were kept entirely secret from other family members and continued well into the patient's teenage years. This was a family that maintained an image of great normalcy before the community. It kept a well-tended lawn, participated in neighborhood life, and regularly attended church. A profound division thus existed between the normal life carried on during the day and the nighttime sexual practices between father and daughter. Once she was old enough to realize that their relationship was not the one all fathers and daughters had, her father instructed her never to speak of their physical intimacy; he explained that other people had not evolved to the point where they could understand what was taking place. He also pressured her to enjoy the sexual episodes, which he said were akin to the practices of royal families during other historical eras. The father told her that what was taking place between them heralded the future of parent–child relations. Her need to comply with his vision of their special relationship was reflected during the period of her psychosis in a delusion that she had been sent to earth by God to have sexual intercourse with all the men on the earth in order to lighten their spirits and lift their gloomy moods. The tie to the mother was also deeply problematic. On one occasion when the patient was six and told her mother something of what had been occurring with her father, she was screamed at and beaten for making up lies. The truth about the incest did not begin to emerge until her midteens, when another child in the family complained about the father's sexual behavior.

During her childhood years, the patient appeared to be a well-adjusted girl. She had many friends, received excellent grades in school, and tried to make her parents proud. The only sign of difficulty she showed was a tendency toward daydreaming, which her teachers and parents encouraged her to curb. Cordoning off the nighttime experiences of sexual molestation and blocking from awareness the destructive impact of these experiences, she consciously identified with the talented, normal child she was known as. Allowing herself to experience or express the confusing tangle of emotions occasioned by the incest threatened her ties to the people closest to her, notably her mother and father. As will be seen, a clear consciousness of what was transpiring also had a disintegrating effect on her sense of her own selfhood.

Hints of the nature of the effects of her situation, however, made an appearance in her recurring dreams. Two repeating nightmares haunted her early and middle childhood years, dreams that were elucidated only many years later as part of her psychotherapy. In one dream she stood in the kitchen of her family's home and noticed the presence of strange dark spots on the floor. Above each spot, any object or part of an object vanished and was annihilated. Observing this, she was terrified to see that the dark spots were beginning to expand, leaving less and less area in the light. In the dream she began to step and jump awkwardly between the growing spots in a desperate effort to avert her own annihilation. This dream emerged during the therapeutic sessions as a child's expression in metaphorical

symbols of the increasing threat to her psychological survival
that she was experiencing in her family. In the second recurrent
dream, she lay prostrate as her body was pulled alternately in
opposite directions by two arrays of strings with little hooks on
them caught under her skin. Small elf-like creatures pulled on
these strings, stretching her skin first in one direction and then
in the other direction. This dream came to be understood as
concretizing the contradictory pulls on her sense of her own self
by her two fathers: one, the loving, responsible father of the
daylight world; and the other, the leering sexual abuser who
inhabited her nights. Here we find an additional and perhaps
even more central motive for her separating off and repressing
so much of the incest experience. To the extent that she remained conscious of all that was taking place in the home,
during the night as well as the day, she faced the threat of being
pulled apart and ultimately ripped into pieces by the contradic-
tions that had been imposed upon her.

Let us return now to the dream that is the focus of our discussion and examine it from the standpoint of the distinctions
between the various forms of unconsciousness. The dynamic
unconscious in this case, consisting in sectors of experience that
have been sacrificed in order to safeguard needed ties and protect
a sense of self-integrity, is represented in the dream by the
underground material that lay beneath the outhouse. The dream
actually portrays not the dynamic unconscious, but rather a
breakdown of repression and the invasion of consciousness by
what earlier was dynamically unconscious. In terms of the patient's life, we could say that the contents of the dynamic
unconscious here consisted principally of the overwhelming
affects generated by her situation in her family, affects that were
never fully articulated or communicated to anyone.

The prereflective unconscious in the dream appears in the
geometry of the imagery, wherein there is a spatial division
between the world above – the daylight, public, conscious realm
of a loving family – and the world below – the nighttime, mostly
unconscious life of betrayal and incest. A profound and central
invariant principle organizing the patient's subjective universe
pertained to this dichotomy, according to which vitally needed
acceptance by others is gained and protected through the sys-

tematic driving underground of one's own emotional truths. The outhouse in the dream, a symbolic receptacle for such unacceptable contents, provided a channel for expunging those areas of her subjective life that threatened the integrity of the daytime world of her family.

The unvalidated unconscious appears in the dream in the undifferentiated, unidentifiable nature of the glowing material that erupted from the toilet. What came up, it will be recalled, was not specific objects that could be identified and labeled, and that would have corresponded to a set of specifically articulated feelings and memories. It was, rather, an overwhelming mass of something she did not recognize. The experiences it had been necessary for this patient to eliminate from her conscious life had never been acknowledged or validated by anyone; indeed, they had been specifically invalidated by both parents: by the father when he redefined the incest as a special rite and insisted that she enjoy it, and by the mother when she angrily punished her daughter for making up lies. This patient, at the outset of her treatment, did not have what one could call emotional knowledge of what had happened to her. She was cognitively aware of the incest, though not of its vast extent, but she had no feeling that she had been victimized, abused, or exploited. Likewise she knew that her mother had ignored her situation, but she had never experienced a sense of betrayal or abandonment by her mother. The exploration of the patient's history within the validating context of the analytic dialogue resulted in the emergence, element by element, in a process extending over nearly two decades, of a more complete emotional sense of the devastating position she had occupied in her family. Of great assistance in the exploration was a detailed investigation of the various delusions and hallucinations she developed during the period of her psychosis, which seemed to encode or otherwise be associated with previously unconscious features of her traumatic history, features that had been submerged in her accommodation to her parents' needs. The result of this illumination was a gradual redefinition of her identity to incorporate the felt reality of having been victimized, exploited, and betrayed as the central experiences of her childhood.

The dynamic unconscious and the unvalidated unconscious

coincide with one another in this case; the patient's repressed emotional reactions to her family situation were parts of experiences that had never been validated by anyone during her childhood years. What emerged from repression at the onset of her psychotic episode was not clear memories and feelings, which could then perhaps have been integrated into her conscious life; her experience at that time was, instead, one of being flooded by disorganizing emotional impressions that she could not understand or articulate. Although sharp distinctions between the different forms of unconsciousness can be drawn theoretically, in the realm of clinical reality, as this case illustrates, the different forms are likely to become manifest in intricately amalgamated ways.

Chapter 3

The Mind and the Body

THE FOCUS OF THIS CHAPTER IS THE RELATIONSHIP between mind and body. The mind–body problem, considered as a metaphysical question, has a long and complicated history within philosophy and many proposed solutions – materialism, idealism, parallelism, interactionism (see Wallace, 1988, for an overview). Classical psychoanalysis has adopted a materialist solution, assigning ontological priority to physical matter – the body and its "drives" – and interpreting the organization of experience as a secondary expression of bodily events. Concepts derived from natural science are reified, and experience is seen as an epiphenomenon of those reifications. Materialist doctrine, with its inevitable reifications, lends itself nicely to the myth of the isolated mind.

Our concern here is the relationship between mind and body in experience. We thus eschew the philosopher's consideration of these terms as referents for any kind of absolutes or tangibly existing entities; nor do we discuss mind and body as terms of linguistic discourse. The inquiry centers instead on mind and body as poles or elements of self-experience and on the varied forms in awareness that the mind-body relationship may take. Hidden in this field of insoluble philosophical controversy is a set of profoundly significant psychological research problems

41

concerning the nature and determining conditions of the different relationships that may exist in experience between mind and body.

We seek both a description of the major variations of the subjective relationship between the mind and the body and a characterization of the specific intersubjective context that is associated with each form of this relationship that is considered. By pursuing this theme, we hope to shed light on the psychological foundations of one of the great problems of metaphysical philosophy and to contribute as well to an expanded understanding of this central dimension of human self-experience.

THE EXPERIENCE OF AFFECT

Our thesis here is that the boundaries between the subjectively experienced mind and body are products of specific, formative intersubjective contexts. One domain in which this can be clearly demonstrated is the experience of affect. In the realm of affective experience, the boundary separating mind and body originates in intersubjective situations closely similar to those in which the division between conscious and unconscious takes form. Indeed, as we shall see, in the affective domain these two experiential boundaries are in large part coextensive.

Krystal (1988) has suggested that a critical dimension of affective development is the evolution of affects from their early form, in which they are experienced as bodily sensations, into subjective states that can gradually be verbally articulated. He also emphasizes the role of the caregiver's ability to identify correctly and verbalize the child's early affects in contributing to this maturational process. Empathically attuned verbal responsiveness fosters the gradual integration of bodily affective experiences into symbolically encoded meanings, leading eventually to the crystalization of distinct feelings. The extent to which a person comes to experience affects as mind (i.e., as feelings) rather than solely as body thus depends on the presence of a facilitative intersubjective context.

In the absence of a facilitating context, derailments of this transformational process occur, whereby affects continue to be experienced primarily as bodily states. The boundary thereby established between mind and body is such that the experiential territory covered by the body remains comparatively large, encompassing affect states that ordinarily come to be experienced as more prominently mental. This situation can be seen as coming about in ways that closely parallel two forms of unconsciousness discussed in chapter 2. On one hand, corresponding to the origins of the unvalidated unconscious, affects may fail to evolve from bodily states to feelings because, in the absence of validating responsiveness, they are never able to become symbolically articulated. Hence, the person remains literally alexithymic (Krystal, 1988). On the other hand, corresponding to the formation of the dynamic unconscious, when a child regularly perceives that his affective experiences are intolerable or injurious to a caregiver, then the symbolic articulation of affect may become blocked or "dispersed" (McDougall, 1989) in order to safeguard the needed bond. The persistence of psychosomatic states and disorders in adults may be understood as remnants of arrests in affective development. When there is an expectation that more advanced, symbolically elaborated feelings will be ignored, will be rejected, or will damage a tie, replicating the faulty attunement of the childhood surround, the person reverts to more archaic, exclusively somatic modes of affective experience and expression (Socarides and Stolorow, 1984/85).[1] In the psychoanalytic situation, when the analyst becomes reliably established in the transference as an attuned, accepting, affect-articulating presence, the psychosomatic symptoms tend to recede or disappear, only to recur or intensify when the therapeutic bond becomes disrupted or when the patient's confidence in the analyst's receptivity to or understanding of his affective states becomes significantly shaken.

THE CONCRETIZATION OF EXPERIENCE

A second set of interrelationships between the subjectively experienced mind and body becomes unveiled through a consider-

---

[1]Certain psychosomatic symptoms may develop when even the bodily component of affective experience is blocked.

ation of the psychological process that we (Atwood and Stolorow, 1984) have termed concretization – the encapsulation of
configurations of subjective experience by concrete, sensorimotor symbols. Concretizations may serve an array of psychological purposes (e.g., wish-fulfilling, self-punishing, adaptive,
defensive, restitutive), but their most general, supraordinate
function is to dramatize, reify, and thereby maintain the organization of the subjective world. The concretization of experience
is a ubiquitous and fundamental process in human psychological
life, underlying a great variety of psychological activities and
products. Concretization can assume a number of forms, depending on what pathways or modes of expression it favors. In
dreams and fantasies, for example, perceptual imagery is employed to actualize required configurations of experience. When
action predominates in the mode of concretization, then behav-
ioral enactments are relied upon to maintain the organization of
experience.

Concretization can mediate the relationship between mind
and body in a number of ways. One such relationship is illustrated by certain sexual enactments, in which intense bodily
experiences are relied on to restore or sustain a precarious, frag-
mentation-prone psychological organization (Kohut, 1971;
Goldberg, 1975; Stolorow and Lachmann, 1980; Socarides,
1988). In a previous work (Atwood and Stolorow, 1984), we
discussed this phenomenon from the standpoint of the contribution of early psychosexual experiences to the development of
the subjective world and of the sense of self in particular. We
contended that the sensual experiences and fantasies that occur
in the course of early development may be viewed as psychic
organizers that contribute importantly to the structuralization of
the sense of self. Specifically, psychosexual experiences provide
the child with an array of sensorimotor and anatomical symbols
that concretize and solidify developmental steps in the articulation of his subjective universe. When these developments are
seriously impeded, leading to structural deficits and weaknesses,
the person may as an adult continue to look to psychosexual
symbols to maintain the organization of his subjective life. By
dramatically enacting these concrete, symbolic forms to the
accompaniment of orgasm, he gives vividly reified, tangible

substance to his efforts to restore a failing sense of self. In such instances, contrary to what Freud (1905) maintained, it is not the infantile erotic experience per se that has been fixated and then regressively reanimated. Instead, it is the early function of the erotic experience that is retained and regressively relied upon – its function in maintaining the cohesion and stability of a sense of self menaced with disintegration. Analytic exploration of the details of sexual enactments, their origins and functions, should reveal the particular ways in which they both encapsulate the danger to the self and embody a concretizing effort at self-restoration.

In sexual and other physical enactments, the body is used in the service of mind, substantializing a needed experience but not substituting for it. In conversion symptoms, by contrast, concrete symbolization creates a bodily substitute for some conflictual experience and thereby modifies the boundary between mind and body in a manner similar to what occurs in psychosomatic states. The conversion – a "symbol written in the sand of the flesh" (Lacan, 1953, p. 69) – enlarges the experience of body at the expense of mind. The intersubjective situations giving rise to conversion symptoms may be quite similar to those in which some psychosomatic states occur, wherein the verbal articulation of affective experience is prevented because it would threaten a needed tie. Unlike psychosomatic states, however, which follow presymbolic pathways of affect expression, conversion symptoms are mediated by symbolic processes. They express in concrete, anatomical symbols what one believes must not be said or will not be heard, beliefs that, in analysis, become a focus of intensive investigation and interpretation.

Whereas psychosomatic and conversion symptoms ordinarily entail alterations in bodily functions, such alterations are not present in hypochondriacal states. In these, the concretization process results in the formation of anxiety-ridden fantasies about the body, in which its parts are pictured as diseased or deteriorating. In the imagery of failing body parts, concrete anatomical symbols are being employed to dramatize and signal an impending psychological catastrophe – the threat of self-disintegration (Kohut, 1971; Stolorow and Lachmann, 1980). The origins of such states can be found in intersubjective situations in which the basic cohesion of self-experience is severely compromised, a subject to which we now turn.

EMBODIMENT, UNEMBODIMENT, AND DISEMBODIMENT

A central constituent of cohesive selfhood is the subjective experience of embodiment, what Winnicott (1945, 1962) refers to as "indwelling." With the achievement of indwelling, the skin becomes the subjective boundary between self and nonself and, experientially, the psyche is felt to reside within the soma. Contributions to this state of unity of mind and body are made in early psychological development by the handling and holding of the child's body (Winnicott, 1945, 1962), by the sensual and other stimulations of the child's body surface that occur within the early child–caregiver interactions (Hoffer, 1950; Mahler, Pine, and Bergman, 1975; Krueger, 1989), and by a variety of early mirror and mirrorlike experiences (Lacan, 1949; Winnicott, 1967; Kohut, 1971, 1977).

The caregiver's responses to the infant's affect states play an especially central role in promoting mind–body cohesion. As we have noted, early affective experiences are, for the most part, a matter of physical sensations rather than psychologically elaborated feelings, and the caregiver's affect attunement is communicated primarily through holding and other sensorimotor contacts with the infant's body. Early deficits in such attunement show themselves in various deformations of the child's body-self and/or in an incomplete attainment of the sense of indwelling. Mind–body unity remains linked to a sustaining selfobject milieu throughout the life cycle, although the child's developing use of symbols and images increasingly obviates the need for immediate sensorimotor attunements and concrete mirroring in order to maintain this aspect of self-cohesion.

The formative contexts of extreme states of disconnection of mind and body typically involve profound failures of early affect attunement, damaging physical intrusions, deprivation of contact needs, and felt threats to physical survival. One can distinguish two general classes of experiences involving a radical separation of mind and body: (1) those reflecting an initial failure to achieve the sense of psychosomatic indwelling, a failure that leaves the person vulnerable to states of severe depersonalization and mind–body disintegration (Winnicott, 1945, 1962; Stolorow and Lachmann, 1980), including dramatic out-of-body "journeys" (see Atwood and Stolorow, 1984, chap. 4, for a detailed case study) and (2) those reflecting active disidentification with the body in order to protect oneself from dangers and conflicts associated with continuing embodied existence. The intersubjective context of the former class is characterized by deficits of early affect attunement, along with destructive intrusions. The context of the latter is more variable, depending on the specific danger that the disidentification with the body serves to avert. These dangers may include immediate threats to the physical self, as in traumatic, near-death experiences (Lifton, 1976), and dangers posed by other persons who are perceived as threats to the psychological survival of the self (Laing, 1960; Winnicott, 1960).

Between the polar extremes of psychosomatic indwelling and complete unembodiment or disembodiment, one may distinguish intermediate forms of disturbance of mind–body cohesion. In one of these, often observed in cases of childhood sexual abuse, there is a sense that the mind is somehow floating outside or above the body, but a complete split between the two does not develop. Here the separation of mind from body may be seen as a less extreme form of defensive disidentification, wherein an attempt is made to protect the integrity of the self through its removal from the field of bodily violation and intrusion. A still less extreme form of disunity is illustrated by experiential states in which the mind is localized in the person's head, retaining its own distinct separateness from the rest of the body. Such a split, which often is expressed as a division between head and body, tends to arise as a defensive organization when there are unbearable conflicts over the expression of "bodily" needs and longings (for tenderness, sexual contact, etc.) in what is felt to be a fundamentally unresponsive, rejecting world. In such instances, the body and its needs tend to be experienced as defective and repugnant to others, the defective body concretizing the rejected, unacceptable self.

A third group of experiences exemplifying an intermediate level of disunity of mind and body involves a person's identification with some external, usually critical viewpoint on the self, an identification so complete that the sense of the self as an embodied subjectivity is eclipsed by an externally situated view of self-as-object. The developmental context of these subjective states does not involve direct threats to the integrity of the self but rather is characterized by interactions in which the child's ability to maintain secure connections to caregiving others was made contingent on meeting stringent standards and expectations imposed from without. In the hope of safeguarding a needed tie to the caregiver, the child here abandons his own unmirrored experience and embraces an outside perspective in its place. This accommodation may result in a sense of being located outside one's body; the body then becomes the focus of critical scrutiny and evaluation and often of intense shame and self-consciousness.

CONCLUSIONS

Our conception of the mind–body dialectic falls broadly within the relational perspective delineated by Mitchell (1988), in that we view the various boundaries and relationships forming between the subjectively experienced mind and body as taking shape in specific relational contexts. The mind–body dialectic can never be understood in isolation; it is always a property of a "living system" (Sander, 1985). This conceptualization holds important implications for the specific framing of psychoanalytic interventions in the clinical situation and also for future investigations of the psychological underpinnings of the various metaphysical solutions to the mind–body problem found in philosophy.

The analytic approach to the various mind–body relationships must take into account what is understood about the differing intersubjective contexts in which they crystalize. In the analysis of psychosomatic disorders or conversion symptoms originating in early situations in which the verbal articulation of affective experience was blocked in order to protect a needed tie, a principal focus of investigation and interpretation will be the patient's expectations or fears in the transference that his emerging feeling states will meet with the same pathogenic reactions from the analyst that they evoked from the original caregiver. An important aspect of such investigation is the delineation of the patient's perceptions of qualities or activities of the analyst that for the patient signal the analyst's intolerance of affect. In contrast, such resistance analysis will not be prominent in the analytic approach to psychosomatic states that reflect the failure of affects to evolve from bodily states to feelings because of the absence of validating responsiveness from the childhood surround. Here the analyst's principal function will be to help lift the patient's affective experience to higher levels of organization by facilitating its articulation in verbal symbols – an example of what we have termed the self-delineating selfobject function.

In the analysis of sexual enactments, hypochondriacal fantasies, and profound states of mind-body disintegration, the analyst will investigate the psychological injuries or the disruptions of archaic ties, past and present, that have compromised the basic cohesion of the patient's self-experience. Concomitantly, the patient will be permitted gradually to form a transforming selfobject bond with the analyst, through which the integrity of the patient's self-experience can eventually come to rest on a more secure foundation. In contrast, when disidentification with the body serves a protective purpose, the analytic investigation will increasingly focus on the patient's feeling of endangerment in the transference, as he anticipates that exposing to the analyst sequestered and vulnerable regions of his self-experience will evoke obliterating intrusions, stony unresponsiveness, or searing criticism.

It seems to us that the various mind–body relationships that occur in experience correspond in a general way to the various solutions to the mind–body problem that have been proposed philosophically. The philosophical doctrine of materialism, for example, resembles the mind–body relationship found in psychosomatic states and conversion symptoms, in that the primacy of the body is affirmed and its domain of influence is greatly enlarged in comparison to that of the mind. Idealist doctrine, in contrast, is similar to unembodied or disembodied states, in that the eternal forms of the mind reign supreme, with the realm of the body being reduced to a mere shadow. Parallelism may correspond to intermediate forms of mind–body disunity wherein mind and body are felt to exist on different planes or in separate locations, whereas interactionism may speak to a greater degree of mind–body integration. The personal, subjective origins of various solutions to philosophical problems are a fascinating area for future psychoanalytic research. From this standpoint, investigations of the intersubjective contexts of mind–body relationships can be seen as a prologue to the psychological study of metaphysical issues.

A number of the mind–body relationships delineated here are illustrated by the case of Jessica in chapter 5.

Chapter 4

Trauma and Pathogenesis

THE CONCEPT OF TRAUMA has remained a pillar of psychoanalytic thought since Freud's (Breuer and Freud, 1893–95)
early studies of the origins of hysteria. Even after Freud (1914)
abandoned the "seduction theory," concluding that "[i]f hysterical subjects trace back their symptoms to traumas that are
fictitious, then the new fact which emerges is precisely that they
create such scenes in *phantasy*" (p. 17), he continued to grant
trauma a central role in pathogenesis. Nevertheless, his conceptualization of trauma was thereafter tilted in a fateful direction,
from trauma as caused by external events to trauma as produced
by forces from within. As Krystal (1988) has pointed out, two
distinct models of psychic trauma were already present in *Studies
on Hysteria*. In one, trauma was the product of an unbearable,
overwhelming affect state; in the other, it was caused by the
emergence of an unacceptable idea, such as a fantasy. Later,
Freud (1926) attempted to reconcile these opposing models by
conceptualizing trauma in terms of the ego's helplessness in the
face of mounting instinctual tensions, whether these were provoked from without or prompted from within. Signal anxiety
and defenses were seen as being mobilized to prevent a psychoe-
conomic catastrophe. Thus, as Freud's theory of the mind
evolved, his conception of trauma increasingly became absorbed

into an unremitting intrapsychic determinism (Stolorow and Atwood, 1979), culminating in the reified image of an isolated, faltering mental apparatus, unable to process the instinctual energies flooding it from within its own depths.

This isolated-mind conception of psychic trauma, emphasizing quantities of instinctual excitation overloading the capacities of an energy processing apparatus, has persisted within Freudian ego psychology (e.g., Kris, 1956). It was retained as well in Kohut's (1971) early attempt to distinguish "optimal frustrations," which promote psychological development, from the traumatic frustrations that result in self-pathology. In a critique of Kohut's conceptualization, one of us, in a chapter written in collaboration with Daphne Stolorow (Stolorow et al., 1987), wrote:

> We are objecting here to the concept of "optimal frustration" because of its retention of economic and quantitative metaphors that are remnants of drive theory. For example, when Kohut (1971) describes an optimal frustration of the child's idealizing need as one in which "the child can experience disappointments with one idealized aspect or quality of the object after another" (p. 50) rather than with the total object, or one in which the shortcomings of the object "are of tolerable proportions" (p. 64), he places the emphasis on the "size" of the disappointment–and, by implication, the "amount" of the depressive affect–as the decisive factor that determines whether the disappointment will be pathogenic or growth-enhancing. In contrast, we are claiming that what is decisive is the responsiveness of the milieu to the child's depressive (and other) reactions. We are thus shifting the emphasis from "optimal frustration" to the centrality of affect attunement [pp. 75–76, fn.].

In agreement with Krystal (1988), it is our view that the essence of trauma lies in the experience of unbearable affect. As was implied in the preceding quotation, however, the intolerability of an affect state cannot be explained solely, or even primarily, on the basis of the quantity or intensity of the painful feelings evoked by an injurious event. As we emphasized in chapter 1, the child's affective experience is a property of, and is regulated within, the child–caregiver system. Developmentally, traumatic affect states must be understood in terms of the relational system in which they take form. Our central thesis in this chapter is that early developmental trauma originates within a formative intersubjective context whose central feature is a failure of affect attunement – a breakdown of the child–caregiver system of mutual regulation – leading to the child's loss of affect-regulatory capacity and thereby to an unbearable, overwhelmed, disintegrated, disorganized state (see Socarides and Stolorow, 1984/85; Stolorow et al., 1987). Painful or frightening affect becomes traumatic, we contend, when the requisite attuned responsiveness that the child needs from the surround to assist in its tolerance, containment, modulation, and alleviation is absent.

The relational context of trauma was recognized by Balint (1969), who postulated three phases contributing to its occurrence in childhood. First, a child is dependent on a trusted adult. Second, this adult proves to be unreliable through overstimulation or neglect and rejection of the child. In the third and crucial phase, the child attempts to "get some understanding, recognition, and comfort" (p. 432) from the adult who perpetrated the disruption. The adult, however, refuses to acknowledge the disturbance, denies that excitement or rejection occurred, often blames the child for his distress, and rejects as well his efforts to seek a trusting reconnection.

A similar conceptualization of developmental trauma, using the framework of psychoanalytic self psychology and emphasizing the fate of the child's painful affect states within the developmental system, has been offered by one of us (Stolorow, in press):

> Most patients who come to us for analysis have, as children, suffered repeated, complex experiences of selfobject failure, which I conceptualize schematically as occurring in two phases. In the first phase, a primary selfobject need is met with rebuff or disappointment by a caregiver, producing a painful emotional reaction. In the second phase, the child experiences a secondary selfobject longing for an attuned response that would modulate, contain, and ameliorate his painful reactive affect state. But parents who repeatedly rebuff primary selfobject needs are usually not able to provide attuned responsiveness to the child's painful

emotional reactions. The child perceives that his painful reactive feelings are unwelcome or damaging to the caregiver and must be defensively sequestered in order to preserve the needed bond. Under such circumstances . . . these walled-off painful feelings become a source of lifelong inner conflict and vulnerability to traumatic states, and in analysis their reexposure to the analyst tends to be strenuously resisted.

It cannot be overemphasized that injurious childhood experiences–losses, for example–in and of themselves need not be traumatic (or at least not lastingly so) or pathogenic, provided that they occur within a responsive milieu (Shane and Shane, 1990). Pain is not pathology. It is the absence of adequate attunement and responsiveness to the child's painful emotional reactions that renders them unendurable and thus a source of traumatic states and psychopathology. This conceptualization holds both for discrete, dramatic traumatic events and for the more subtle "impingements" (Winnicott, 1949), overstimulations (Greenacre, 1958), or narcissistic woundings (Kohut, 1971), the "silent traumas" (Hoffer, 1952) or "cumulative traumas" (Khan, 1963) that occur continually throughout childhood. Whereas Khan (1963) conceptualized cumulative trauma as the "result of the breaches in the mother's role as a protective shield over the whole course of the child's development" (p. 46), we understand such ongoing trauma more in terms of the failure to respond adequately to the child's painful affect once the "protective shield" has been breached. As Kohut (1971) repeatedly emphasized, such cumulative trauma often results from specific character pathology in the parent, whose narcissistic use of the child, for example, precludes the recognition of, acceptance of, and attuned responsiveness to the child's painful reactive affect states. Indeed, images depicting discrete, dramatic trauma, whether derived from memories of events, fantasies, or both in some combination, often metaphorically encode these more subtle, recurrent early interaction patterns involving pervasive emotional exploitation of, and malattunement to, the child (Stolorow et al., 1987).

Lacking an affect-integrating, containing, and modulating intersubjective context, the traumatized child must dissociate the painful affect from his ongoing experiencing, often resulting in psychosomatic states or in splits between the subjectively experienced mind and body (chapter 3), or withdrawal behind a protective shield or cocoon (Modell, 1976), safe from potential injuries that would result from attachments to others. Even if able to remember the traumatogenic experiences, the child may remain plagued by tormenting doubts about their actuality, or even about the reality of his experience in general (chapter 1), an inevitable consequence of the absence of validating attunement that we are contending lies at the heart of psychic trauma. The traumatized child will fail to develop the capacity for affect tolerance and the ability to use affects as information-providing signals; and painful affects, when felt, will tend to engender traumatic states (Socarides and Stolorow, 1984/85; Stolorow et al., 1987; Krystal, 1988). Such a child may feel compelled to renounce "imagining, hoping, and wishing for what is possible, all of which have only brought unbearable vulnerability and tremendous frustration" (Shabad, 1989, p. 118) and may develop a " 'doomsday orientation,' that is, profound pessimism frequently accompanied by chronic fears and depressive lifestyle" (Krystal, 1988, p. 148).

In general, it may be said that *"[d]evelopmental traumata derive their lasting significance from the establishment of invariant and relentless principles of organization that remain beyond the . . . influence of reflective self-awareness or of subsequent experience"* (Brandchaft and Stolorow, 1990, p. 108). The traumatized child, for example, may "conclude" that his own unmet needs and emotional pain are expressions of disgusting and shameful defects in the self and thus must be banished from conscious experiencing; he, in effect, blames his own reactive states for the injuries that produced them. The establishment of such organizing principles, which often entails wholesale substitution of the caregiver's subjective reality for the child's own (see the case of Jessica, chapter 5; also Brandchaft, 1991), both preserves the tie to the injurious or inadequately responsive caregiver and protects against retraumatization. Once formed, such principles, which usually operate unconsciously (chapter 2), acutely sensitize the traumatized person to any subsequent experience that lends itself to being interpreted as an actual or impending repetition of the original trauma, necessitating the mobilization of defensive activity (Ornstein, 1974). Retraumatization later in life occurs when there is a close replication of the original trauma, a confirmation of the organizing principles that resulted from the original trauma,[1] or a loss or disruption of a sustaining bond that has provided an alternative mode of organizing experience, without which the old invariant principles are brought back into the fore.

Nowhere is the doctrine of the isolated mind more deleterious than in the conceptualization of trauma. Despite Ferenczi's (1933) early attempt to redress the neglect of abuse, particularly sexual abuse, in the pathogenesis of the neuroses and his suggestion that analysts actually reproduce the original trauma in their blunders and blindnesses, it is only in recent years that the frequent sexual and other physical abuse of children has been systematically addressed by psychoanalysts (e.g., Miller, 1986; Levine, 1990; Kramer and Akhtar, 1991). To attribute the affective chaos or schizoid withdrawal of patients who were abused as children to "fantasy" or to "borderline personality organizations" is tantamount to blaming the victim and, in so doing, reproduces features of the original trauma. The assumption that trauma is produced by the child's failure to channel drive energies arising from within, rather than by the relational creation of intolerable excitement, pain, and feelings of helplessness, has been paralleled in classical psychoanalysis's explanation of negative transferences and resistances in terms of intrapsychic mechanisms located solely within the patient. Just as the abused child could not blame his parents because of his need for them, and therefore felt compelled to repress or disavow the experiences of abuse, it is likely that, without the analyst's help, the traumatized patient will feel compelled to suppress his awareness of disruptions in the analysis or to blame himself for their occurrence, thereby attempting to survive the traumas of analysis as he had the traumas of childhood.

Both Winnicott (1963) and Kohut (1959) stressed the crucial therapeutic importance of recognizing and acknowledging the

---

[1]This pathway to retraumatization was helpfully clarified in discussions with Claudia Kohner.

validity, from within the patient's perspective, of the reexperiencing of traumatogenic developmental failure in the transference:

> The reaction to the current [analytic] failure . . . makes sense
> insofar as the current failure *is* the original environmental failure
> from the point of view of the child [Winnicott, 1963, p. 209].

> [For the severely traumatized patient,] the analyst is not the
> screen for the projection of internal structure . . . but the direct
> continuation of an early reality that was too distant, too reject-
> ing, or too unreliable. . . . [The analyst] *is* the old object with
> which the analysand tries to maintain contact [Kohut, 1959, pp.
> 218–219].

Anyone who has used the clinical concepts of psychoanalytic
self psychology in conducting a psychoanalysis has witnessed
the therapeutic benefits of analyzing disruptions experienced
within the analytic bond. Throughout his writings, Kohut
(1971, 1977, 1984) explained these therapeutic effects by in-
voking his theory of optimal frustration leading to transmuting
internalization, a formulation that, as we noted earlier, incorpo-
rates classical metapsychology's quantitative and mechanistic
metaphors, relics of the doctrine of the isolated mind. We believe that the therapeutic impact of analyzing disruptions is
better explained in the light of the traumatized patient's history
of absent or inadequate affect attunement. In conducting such an
analysis, the analyst investigates and interprets the various elements of the rupture from within the patient's subjective frame
of reference – the qualities or activities of the analyst that produced the disruption, the principles that organized its meanings, its impact on the analytic bond and on the patient's self-
experience, the early developmental trauma it replicated, and,
especially important, the patient's expectations and fears of how
the analyst will respond to the articulation of the painful feelings that followed in its wake (Stolorow et al., 1987). In our
view, it is the transference meaning of this investigative and
interpretive activity that is its principal source of therapeutic
action; it establishes the analyst in the transference as the sec-
ondarily longed-for, receptive, understanding parent who,

through his attuned responsiveness, will "hold" (Winnicott, 1954) and thereby eventually alleviate the patient's painful emotional reaction to an experience of repetition of early developmental failure. The analytic bond becomes thereby mended and expanded, and primary developmental yearnings are permitted to emerge more freely as the patient feels increasing confidence that his emotional reactions to experiences of rebuff and disappointment will be received, understood, and contained by the analyst. Concomitantly, a developmental process is set in motion wherein the formerly sequestered painful reactive affect states, the heritage of the patient's history of developmental trauma, gradually become integrated and transformed and the patient's capacity for affect tolerance becomes increasingly strengthened.

The emotional intensity of the analytic relationship, in remobilizing thwarted developmental longings and painful emotional vulnerabilities in the transference, is fertile ground for potential retraumatizations of the patient. It is our view that the fear or anticipation of retraumatization by the analyst is central to the phenomenon of resistance in psychoanalysis. The fear of retraumatization may be evoked merely by the analyst's bodily presence or by his benign interest in knowing the patient's experience, the latter of which raises the spectre of humiliating exposure and searing shame. This dread of exposure, which can be provoked by the analytic process no matter how "empathic" and accepting the analyst perceives himself to be, is dramatically illustrated by an analytic dream recently reported by Bromberg (1991):

> In the dream, the analyst, undisguised and with an earnest manner and a genuinely warm smile, throws into the patient's lap a bag containing a two-headed monster. The patient is terrified because she knows she is expected to open the bag, but she *cannot tell the analyst how frightened she is because the monster will just get larger* [p. 401, fn., emphasis added].

We infer from the imagery of this dream that this patient expects her analyst to respond to the exposure of her escalating painful feelings with the same malattunement they received from her original caregivers, thereby reinvoking the original childhood trauma and the view of herself as a loathsome monster that resulted.

What we wish to emphasize is that a patient's need to wall himself off from his own affectivity, from his yearnings for connection with the analyst, and from the analyst's interpretations is *always* evoked by perceptions of qualities or activities of the analyst that *lend themselves* to the patient's fears or anticipations of a repetition of childhood trauma. It is essential to the analysis of resistance that this be recognized, investigated, and interpreted by the analyst.

Our conceptualization of trauma and pathogenesis, and its implications for the analysis of resistance, are well illustrated by the case of Jessica in the next chapter.

Chapter 5

Fantasy Formation

(written in collaboration with Daphne S. Stolorow)

F REUD (1900) USED THE TERM *fantasy* to refer to daydreams, conscious and unconscious, and noted their similarity to night dreams. Fantasies, like dreams, cast configurations of experience into concrete perceptual images. Fantasies can subserve the entire gamut of psychological functions encountered in clinical psychoanalytic work – wish-fulfilling, defensive, self-punishing, and so on. We emphasize the specific function of fantasy in intersubjective situations wherein powerful affective experiences fail to evoke adequate validating responses from the surround. In such instances, the concrete sensorimotor images of the fantasy dramatize and reify the person's emotional experience, conferring upon it a sense of validity and reality that otherwise would be absent. An analogous function may be served by certain types of enactment through which a person attempts to articulate experiences that could never be encoded symbolically.

As one of many possible examples of this conception of fantasy, consider the archaic grandiose-exhibitionistic fantasies that Kohut (1971) believed were of central importance in the early development of the self. Unlike Kohut, we do not regard these grandiose fantasies as primary developmental building blocks. Rather, it is our view that such fantasies are constructed reactively in situations wherein the child's primary affective

61

experiences of excitement, expansiveness, pride, efficacy, and pleasure in himself fail to evoke the requisite validating responsiveness from caregivers. The concrete imagery of the grandiose fantasy both dramatizes and affirms the unvalidated affective experience and depicts as well what the child perceived was required of him in order to extract the missing responsiveness.[1]

Another class of fantasies that may arise in consequence of the experience of invalidation involves the picturing of the invalidating other as somehow having been taken into one's own mind. Such fantasies, which object relations theorists have designated with the term *introject,* concretize the process whereby regions of invalidity in the child's subjective world are filled in by emotionally significant others. Although the imagery of having an invalidating object within one's own mind may also serve the secondary function of providing an illusion of mastery or control over its usurping power (Fairbairn, 1943), its primary meaning is that it dramatizes the child's inability to maintain the integrity of his own experience in the face of overwhelming pressure from the invalidating other.

A distinction is sometimes drawn between "positive" and "negative" introjects, the former referring to images of internal objects possessing idealized, benign features, and the latter to images emphasizing critical, sadistic, or otherwise destructive features. It has even been suggested that a criterion of psychological health is the possession of one or more positive or "good" internal objects (Klein, 1940). The question may be raised whether so-called positive introjects also exemplify the process whereby regions of invalidity in a person's experience are filled in by others' perceptions and judgments. The essence of introjection, as we are conceptualizing it, lies in the substitution of some part of the psychic reality of an invalidating other for the child's own experience. Such a substitution or filling in could conceivably emphasize quite positive features of the object and yet remain fundamentally a usurpation of the child's subjectivity in that the child feels required to affirm and incorporate these qualities in order to maintain the needed tie to the object.

---

[1] We are grateful to Dr. Bernard Brandchaft for bringing this latter point to our attention.

There are, however, occasions when the fantasy of possessing a good object within one's mind does not concretize an invalidation, but expresses an effort to support an unsteady capacity for self-validation. Here too a substitution is occurring and being concretized, but the portion of the other's psychic reality entering the child's experience contains as its most essential feature the function of validating empathy. Such fantasies are often observed in the course of psychoanalytic therapy when a patient is experiencing the transition from reliance on the bond with the analyst to provide understanding and validation and is beginning to provide these functions for himself.

Daydreams or fantasies, like any content of experience, can undergo repression when they, or the affective states they concretize, are perceived to endanger a tie that is required for psychological survival. However, the concept of unconscious fantasy has been expanded to encompass much more psychological territory than Freud's notion of a repressed or dynamically unconscious daydream. Arlow (1969), for example, after affirming that "the term fantasy . . . is used in the sense of the daydream" (p. 5), describes the role of what he terms "unconscious fantasy" in perception:

> Unconscious fantasy activity provides the "mental set" in which sensory stimuli are perceived and integrated. . . . Under the pressure of [unconscious fantasies] the ego is oriented to scan the data of perception and to select discriminatively from the data of perception those elements that demonstrate some consonance or correspondence with the latent, preformed fantasies [p. 8]. [Unconscious fantasying] supplies the mental set in which the data of perception are organized, judged, and interpreted [p. 23].

As Slap (1987) has implied, such formulations describe not repressed daydreams but the operation of developmentally preformed unconscious *schemata* – that is, psychological structures – into which the person is assimilating his current experiences. The phrase "unconscious fantasy" is being employed imprecisely to refer to the unconscious organizing principles constituting the domain of unconsciousness that we have termed the prereflective unconscious. It is these unconscious ordering principles, formed within the intersubjective matrix of the child-caregiver system, that underlie both the mental sets that organize perception and, when concretized, such phenomena as symptoms, enactments, dreams, and fantasies.

We turn now to a clinical illustration demonstrating the specific, invalidating intersubjective context in which a vivid introject fantasy took form.

THE CASE OF JESSICA

Jessica, an attractive yet somewhat masculine-looking actress, entered psychoanalytic therapy at the age of 26. The difficulties she initially described pertained to painful feelings of jealousy, which created arguments with her boyfriend, and a "not-so-good" feeling about herself that was longstanding. Nevertheless, it soon became clear that she suffered from a variety of emotional and psychosomatic problems. Her disruptive affect states were often experienced somatically as episodic spells of dizziness, fainting, vomiting, and other gastrointestinal symptoms. She had very poor eating habits, would engage in self-destructive behavior, and was unable to sleep normally. Her sleep was disturbed by nightmares that depicted past traumatic events and that continued to disrupt her after she had awakened. She suffered from chronic boredom, persistent anxiety with episodes of panic, and an intense fear of being alone. In general, Jessica showed little capacity for self-care.

Within a few sessions it became apparent that Jessica had been suffering from a serious, chronic depression punctuated by states of emptiness and suicidal thoughts and behavior. Her psychosomatic ailments, anxiety, insomnia, and nightmares exacerbated her depressive states and made her feel that people saw her as "strange and not quite right." One of her initial fears in the transference was that the therapist would see how "bad" she was and would realize that she should not be alive. Thus, Jessica craved reassurance that the therapist both wanted her to live and would take a strong stand to this effect on her behalf. It was learned as the treatment progressed that this initial fear had encapsulated Jessica's essential life struggle, and it persisted as

one of her most painful fears in her relationship with the therapist. Each time the therapist went away for a weekend or on a
vacation, Jessica would interpret the absence as confirmatory
evidence that she should be dead. If the therapist was abandoning their struggle for her life, she concluded, this must mean
that she had no right to be alive.

Jessica's fears became more understandable as aspects of her
inner world unfolded. When the anniversary of an older brother's death approached, for example, she became overtly suicidal.
She was afraid both that she would die and that the therapist's
life also was in danger. Soon it became evident that Jessica
maintained a strong delusional belief that her brother, Justin,
who had died some 12 years prior to the beginning of treatment,
had literally taken over her life in a most profound and fundamental way: Justin had "become part" of her. Not only did he
live within her; she was convinced that she had become he. She
felt she had no distinct identity—Jessica did not really exist.

During the treatment this sense of nonbeing emerged as the
central feature of her self-experience. Each waking hour was
characterized by an endless battle against "the force," as she
referred to her brother within her. She experienced intense and
often prolonged disorganized states in which his being would
take over her psychological and physical functioning. At these
times she would become seriously suicidal and would feel a
wave of anxiety concerning the welfare of those she loved. She
was sure that Justin would rob her of anyone that she truly
cared for. She feared having any interests, likes, or dislikes that
were different from those of her brother, and she felt intensely
guilty about any pleasure or joy that she could envision in her
lifetime. Jessica could not imagine that she would live very long.
Each year she lived past the age at which Justin had died only
intensified her panic and her conviction that her very existence
was a cruel and destructive act that would bring harm to her
family.

Jessica was the youngest of six, born to wealthy parents of
English descent. The family had been well known and respected
in the rather small New England community in which they
lived. Jessica's parents separated when she was under five years
of age, but the father often "pretended" to be part of the family

"for the sake of his reputation." Jessica felt that a good show was always put on for the neighbors, even though "our house was crumbling from within." She portrayed her mother as a hard-driving, compulsive, and anxiety-filled woman who was very concerned with the way things looked to other people. She was quite active socially and was employed, along with Jessica's father, in the import-export business. Jessica's conviction that her mother hated small children and felt burdened by them crystalized around memories of being left at home while the rest of the family went on trips – because she was the youngest and would be too much trouble to care for on a *pleasure* trip.

Jessica's father was very career oriented and spent prolonged periods of time completely engrossed in his work. Even as a young child, Jessica knew of his many extramarital affairs. Because of the nature of their work, her parents were regularly called out of town on business trips that sometimes lasted for months. At such times, Jessica was left at home with an assortment of substitute caretakers. The parents did not call regularly when they were away, nor did they provide accurate information as to when they would return. Each time Jessica had to say goodbye she feared it was for the last time. These separations from her parents began soon after her birth and continued for many years. Not surprisingly, she developed a deep feeling of insecurity and an extreme vulnerability to absences. She also failed to develop a firm sense that she existed in other people's minds when they were not physically present. This remained a powerful source of anxiety for her throughout her development. She could not even imagine the reliable presence of a calming, benign parental figure. The closest she had ever come to such an experience was with her now-deceased brother, Justin, who during his short life gave her a sense of being loved and cared for.

When Jessica was 12 years old, Justin was diagnosed as having a rare and usually fatal disease and for two painful years went through a seemingly endless barrage of treatments. During those years she experienced a sudden loss of Justin, who now had to spend many hours with the doctors, and also of her mother, who threw herself into the ultimately fruitless search for a cure. From the time the disease was discovered until her brother's death, Jessica saw very little of either of them. Her mother would at times reassure her that Justin was really fine and there was no reason to worry, but of course this was contrary to what Jessica perceived. Even the night before Justin's death, her mother was "still swearing that he'd be OK."

Soon after Justin became ill, Jessica was taken out of school for nearly two years to live with her godparents in a small rural community because there was no one else to take care of her. The abrupt and massive deprivations – emotional, intellectual, and social – contributed to her sense that her life completely stopped when Justin became ill. She had only sporadic tutoring by a family friend, and, when she finally returned to school, she was ostracized, laughed at, and, worst of all, feared, because the other children knew of her brother's disease and believed they could catch it from her. This was one in a series of experiences that shaped her delusional conviction that she was Justin.

Jessica's father, who had been quite uninvolved with the family, had a particularly difficult time with Justin's illness. During these years, and for many following Justin's death, the father could not look at Jessica because he perceived such a strong resemblance between her and Justin. Her father thereby showed his inability to experience Jessica as a separate person, distinct from his son. Like the experience of being shunned by her schoolmates, this too contributed to Jessica's delusion that she was Justin. "If your father can't even look at you, there must be a good reason. I reminded him too much of Justin."

The family never talked openly about what was happening to Justin or to the family. As Justin's health worsened and death became imminent, Jessica's parents seemed to picture Justin in ever-more idealized, even godlike terms. At the same time they began to "see" more and more qualities that Jessica and Justin shared in common. Both parents felt that the two children looked more alike than ever before, and even Jessica, who since Justin's illness had been very frightened of being like him, started to become convinced that she really did bear a strong mental and physical resemblance to her older brother. Her mother began to cut Jessica's hair in the same short, blunt style that Justin wore and insisted that Jessica not only sleep in Justin's room but literally make it her own. After that, Jessica was no longer even permitted back in her own room and was expected literally to take Justin's place. After Justin's death, the pressure of these demands to transform herself into her brother became enormous. One week after the funeral the mother switched jobs and left for an extended business trip to Australia, and the father once again dropped out of sight. Jessica remembered that there was absolutely no talk of what had happened and that she slowly became confused about whether it had ever really happened at all. She thus experienced a profound absence of validation – indeed, a relentless disconfirmation – of her own historical experience of her brother's life and of his death. She began to believe, in conformity with her parents' wishes, that Justin had never really died and instead had taken over her mind and body.

Thus began her delusional merger and her lifelong struggle to free herself without killing him. The brother she had loved so dearly had saved himself by living in her body and taking over her being. How could she murder him by asserting, or even experiencing, her distinctness? How could she let him die when she felt that *she* was to blame for his illness? If it hadn't been for her, she thought, Justin would not have been sent away to military school and her mother would have seen the signs of his illness sooner – "perhaps in time to save his life." The mother had felt overwhelmed by the demands of six children, and Jessica, as she was repeatedly told, had become very difficult to handle. Jessica felt that, had she not been so difficult during that period, Justin would not have been sent away and so would still be alive. In fact, Justin on occasion had actually accused her of causing his disease.

Jessica's parents continued to fuel the delusion that their son had been transported into the body and mind of his younger sister. Jessica was, in effect, sacrificed to maintain the denial of their son's death. After Justin's death, all pictures of Jessica were removed from the house, except those in which Jessica showed a striking resemblance to Justin. Additionally, her parents would deny that Jessica had any likes or dislikes that were inconsistent with what Justin had liked or disliked. She felt required to take on all of Justin's qualities, feelings, and thoughts – his favorite food, sport, and even the clothes he liked to wear. Jessica's father refused to see her for many years following the death, which meant to her that he did not see her as a separate person and could not face that he had lost a son. By incorporating and becoming Justin, Jessica protected her parents from the loss they could not tolerate.

Course of Treatment and the Working-Through Process

Jessica's therapy–five sessions per week over a nine-month period–was initially stormy, unpredictable, and marked by numerous crises. She became intensely involved with the therapist from the start and tried desperately to engage her. In the first session Jessica was upset with the therapist for not having more books on the shelves, pictures on the wall, and papers on the desk, because the absence of these articles symbolized for her the constant threat of abandonment. It was as if the therapist were ready to vanish from the office and from Jessica's life without a moment's notice. The more articles that were in the office, the more Jessica would feel temporarily reassured. Hence, from the first hour the therapist saw the emotional results of Jessica's early experiences with loss, abandonment, and inconsistency.

Jessica asked many personal questions of the therapist: Was she married? Did she have children? What was her favorite food? Her favorite color? These questions were later understood to reflect both her need for concrete information to provide a sense of the therapist as real and tangible and the requirement that Jessica become like the person she was with. She felt frustrated whenever her questions were not answered, and this feeling of frustration continued throughout the course of treatment. Later, it was learned that the therapist's failure to answer personal questions was disturbing to Jessica because it repeated early painful experiences of not being included in her parents' "secret lives." As this repetition was clarified and understood, she became increasingly able to tolerate the lack of answers.

During the first week of treatment, after telling the therapist a great deal about her life, Jessica began to express intense fears that the therapist would take over her mind. These fears alternated with worries about being found repugnant and a failure in

and an overwhelming guilt whenever she looked out for
. Sensing Jessica's wrenching conflicts in the area of self-
ntiation, the therapist interpreted these fears as originating in Jessica's fundamental confusion over who she really
was, her guilt over any acts of self-assertion or self-demarcation
and her profound sense of badness whenever she felt or did
something that did not correspond to what she believed was
required of her. These requirements possessed enormous power,
for she believed that the only way to maintain a relationship
was to fulfill the other person's needs – regardless of the violence
such compliance would do to the core of her being.

The principal focus of the early weeks of therapy was Jessica's
sense of self–other confusion and the guilt and ruthless self-
attack that followed any expression of her distinctness. As these
themes were repeatedly clarified, she became flooded with
memories of how her mother would feel injured and then be
rageful and attacking whenever Jessica was not organized
around her needs. Likewise, Jessica believed that now she had to
mold herself to whom and what the therapist needed her to be.
The understanding and interpretation of this requirement as it
emerged in the transference established a foundation of trust
that enabled therapy to proceed.

To illustrate the working-through process, our presentation of
the treatment is organized around five pivotal crises. The understanding and working through of each crisis ushered in a move
toward greater self-differentiation, and each succeeding step toward more differentiated selfhood was more successful than the
one that had come before. These developmental advances led to
a gradual diminution of Jessica's suicidal preoccupations, until
they finally dropped away completely. In describing the five
crises, we focus on how the therapist and the patient began and
maintained the process of Jessica's self-delineation, how the
prohibitions against differentiation were revived in the transference, and how these conflicts and developmental arrests, along
with her unremitting suicidality, were worked through within
the archaic transference bond.

Prior to the first crisis, Jessica had been taking small but
notable steps in her struggle to assert her distinctness. She did so
particularly in her relationship with a woman friend by refusing

to take responsibility for the friend's problems and declaring that she needed things in their relationship too. These seemingly small achievements were of enormous significance to Jessica and produced intense conflicts. She felt an automatic sense of danger and, in consequence, began to disconnect from the stand she had taken with her friend.

The first crisis was a double devastation for Jessica. Her boyfriend, who was in the Armed Services, was suddenly killed in a plane crash, and her father was pronounced missing while on a climbing expedition (he was found in relatively good health two days later). Jessica became hysterical and seriously suicidal. Until this point in treatment her suicidality had remained rather elusive. She had spoken of numerous serious accidents that seemed to indicate suicidal intent, but she had not overtly expressed any wish to terminate her life. Now she was actually expressing a fear of *having* to kill herself, rather than a wish to die. This fear of having to kill herself derived directly from her delusional merger with Justin. She "knew" that Justin was angry with her for the steps she had been taking toward self-demarcation, and she believed that he was taking revenge by bringing harm to people she cared about. He had caused the death of her boyfriend and their father's disappearance, and therefore Jessica felt she would have to commit suicide to save others from his wrath. This feeling alternated with her belief that she was required to be her brother and therefore should be dead as he was. Consequently, Jessica engaged in very dangerous activities and also became terrified that the therapist would die. She could not bear to be alone, and her pleas for personal information became ever more intense. The sessions were filled with Jessica's urgent demands for closeness and for reassurances that the therapist not abandon her, and with further elaborations of her merger experience with Justin.

Jessica's response to the crisis became comprehensible from the vantage point of her archaic inner world. She believed that her attempts at self-assertion with her woman friend had led directly to her boyfriend's death because, as she put it, she "destroyed people" whenever she made any steps toward self-differentiation. Her boyfriend's death and her father's disappearance powerfully confirmed something that she "had known all along"–that any attempt to have a life of her own would lead to disaster. Her self-destructiveness, which included an almost total cessation of eating and chronic involuntary vomiting, was pun-ishment for even being alive. During the crisis, Jessica was unable to maintain any mental image of the therapist, and she felt increasingly anxious as the end of each session approached. She lost all sense of satisfaction in her usual activities and began to center her life entirely on her therapy.

Even with five sessions a week and frequent phone calls during the weekends, Jessica needed to know the whereabouts of the therapist at all times. She was plagued by the fear that she or the therapist would literally disappear if they were not to-gether. Additionally, she believed that Justin would eventually retaliate against the therapist for attempting slowly to separate the two siblings and break up the merger between them. Hence, she desperately needed to feel united with the therapist to main-tain even a rudimentary sense of herself and to stave off retalia-tion from Justin. It was only through the archaic bond to the therapist that she felt safe. When her need for oneness with the therapist became especially urgent, it sometimes seemed to be expressed in an eroticized form, as Jessica came to her sessions in sexually provocative attire. Analytic investigation of this be-havior revealed that erotization of archaic longings for oneness had long been characteristic of her relationships with both males and females.

Other fears at this point concerned what would be left of Jessica if she separated from Justin. Her worst fears stemmed from the experience of a total lack of being–a sense of herself as an empty, disintegrated shell of a person. During this period, her dread of not being remembered by the therapist after she left the sessions became pervasive and overwhelming. She pleaded for reassurance that the therapist would continue to think about her when not in her presence. Only then could she be assured of her own existence in time and space. She asked the therapist to write down something about her on paper so that she would not be forgotten. Yet, all along she feared that the therapist secretly felt she should be dead. This fear seemed confirmed whenever the therapist went away or when Jessica could detect any weariness or exasperation in the therapist's mood, which she constantly monitored.

During separations Jessica would be calmed by phone contacts with the therapist, which helped her to maintain an image of the therapist, along with the desperately needed sense of connection. The separations from the therapist on weekends or holidays produced intense fears of people, fears that the therapist would die, and a loss of any sense of security that may have developed during the preceding week. Jessica would then begin to experience a dawning awareness of how "needy" she was, would degrade herself, and would then become convinced that she was becoming a burden to the therapist as she had sensed she had been to her mother. At these times she would fear that she was all alone in her attempt to separate from Justin and have her own life. The repeated clarification of her fears, however, seemed to calm her somewhat, and, as the crisis slowly abated, she reported a feeling of greater solidity within herself.

The second crisis was brought on by the approaching anniversary of Justin's death. Strong suicidal urges were the most salient feature of this period. These urges were repeatedly interpreted as reflecting her feeling that she "was supposed to be dead" because she was supposed to be Justin and her belief that each day she lived represented a breach of that requirement. Jessica felt that living her own life inflicted a lethal injury on her mother in particular, because the mother's psychological survival seemed to depend on Jessica's sacrificing her life for the "greater cause." The suicidal urges were especially intense now, because she felt that the therapist was firmly committed to helping her separate psychologically from her brother. As the therapist consistently interpreted the prohibition against Jessica's existing as a distinct person, the requirement that she sacrifice herself seemed to lose some of its hold on her. She began to experience the therapist as someone who could be completely aligned with her attempts at self-differentiation, however dangerous such attempts might be. Earlier Jessica had often believed that the therapist wanted her to die, as she believed her mother had; but now, at least temporarily, she felt the therapist's "force" battling against her brother's enormous power. As her suicidal thoughts came to be understood as fears of having to be murdered, this clarified for the patient her essential wish to live and have a life of her own, which helped her enormously during the crisis period. After she recovered from the anniversary, she felt stronger and more able to tolerate separations from the therapist. She was becoming able to create a mental image of the therapist during these separations and to question her belief that the therapist would not return. Still, Jessica would need to ask, "Are you glad I'm still alive?"

For a few days things seemed to settle down. Jessica felt calmer than she had ever been since beginning treatment. The third crisis seemed to result directly from her progress in treatment so far and was marked by the first of many depersonalization experiences. She had been performing at a local theater and during the intermission realized that she was actually enjoying herself—a very rare experience in her life until now, since any enlivening feeling of pleasure represented separation from her dead brother. On realizing her sense of enjoyment, she became increasingly anxious, depressed, and panicky. Suddenly, she could not recall her name, or where she lived, or who her family were, and she became disoriented in time and space. She found a piece of paper in her bag with the therapist's name and phone number on it and, with great trepidation, called her. When she arrived at the office, she was in a disoriented state. Familiar objects and people were now strange and frightening, and she was acutely sensitive to noise. Her panic over not knowing the most basic facts about her life, including the purpose for which she was coming to the therapist, subsided gradually as the therapist calmed her by supplying her with concrete information about her existence. An understanding of why Jessica had become disconnected from herself in such a profound way became the focus of several sessions. For Jessica, even a momentary experience of pleasure, self-confidence, or aliveness came into direct conflict with the merged relationship she felt required to maintain with her brother. At the theater, she began to feel *like herself* and, if only for a moment, she was doing something uniquely her own.

At times during the session that followed her enjoyable performance, Jessica was quite delusional, exclaiming that Justin *really was* alive and that if she separated from him she would kill him. "I can't let him die! He's not dead!" The longed-for state of aliveness and distinctness had produced an acute episode of depersonalization, whose function was to protect the merger with Justin and hence to save his "life." At this point she voiced the idea that the only way she could free herself was to commit suicide (which the depersonalization state symbolically accomplished) because by doing so she could put an end to Justin's existence. But Jessica did not really want to die. Even though Jessica had been suicidal for many years, she and the therapist came to recognize that she had a very strong will to live.

Episodes of depersonalization occurred sporadically during the course of treatment, triggered by Jessica's acts of demarcation from her brother. Gradually, the depersonalizations decreased in frequency and intensity, as the origins, meanings, and functions of the delusional merger, as well as the suicidal preoccupations, became increasingly clarified.

As Jessica recovered from the third crisis, she seemed stronger and better able to think about herself. For the first time in years, she seriously focused on her career. She was now able to tolerate two-day separations from the therapist and to reflect on her own inner states without the therapist having to be present. Her attention to her career had special meaning because it indicated that she felt more permitted to embrace the idea that she could have distinctive interests and goals of her own. During this period Jessica felt the bond with the therapist to be "life sustaining." She felt she could now experiment with her life, but only under the "protective blanket" of the therapeutic bond. This bond had become established as a facilitating medium in which aborted self-differentiating processes could once again be resumed.

Just as things were settling down, Jessica was faced with a five-day separation from the therapist. Since the therapist had become established as the guardian of Jessica's essential selfhood, such a separation produced profound effects. In reaction to the loss of the vitally needed tie, she again became acutely depersonalized. The therapist carefully outlined for Jessica the dangers to which the separation exposed her—that Jessica felt all alone in her struggle for distinctness, that she became increasingly vulnerable to attacks by her brother, and that her parents' requirement that she sacrifice herself returned in all its intensity. In consequence of the separation, Jessica became more vulnerable to slipping back into the merger with Justin. During this period, her dreams often contained imagery dramatizing the traumatic loss of the therapist's protective functions.

Significant changes in Jessica's psychological organization were now taking place as a result of the careful investigation and understanding of how she had been required to renounce her strivings for self-definition. Her reaction to the fourth crisis provided an example of how far Jessica had come in her uphill battle for emotional freedom. She became pregnant and terminated the pregnancy by abortion. With the creation and ending of this new life within her came an array of intense emotional reactions, including extreme anxiety, intolerable guilt, and a profound sense of loss. The abortion reanimated her fantasy that her own angry wishes had caused Justin's death. Not unexpectedly, the transference was also affected by the loss of the fetus. Jessica became afraid that the therapist would now clearly see that she had killed her brother as she had killed her baby and that any further disclosure would inevitably drive the therapist away. After all, as a 12-year-old girl had she not wished that Justin would finally die because he was taking away all of her mother's time, energy, and emotional resources? Jessica's feelings of inherent destructiveness were pervasive, but she *did not become suicidal.* For the first time in 12 years she was able to feel the guilt, the loss, and the despair, without experiencing a conviction that she should die because of another's suffering.

Jessica became immersed in intense guilt and what she called "paranoia." She was afraid of everything and everybody and was unable to take care of the details of her daily life. The budding new sense of herself that had been developing was profoundly shaken, and she imagined that almost anything could harm her. The therapist interpreted these fears as arising both from her guilt over being alive when Justin and the fetus had died and from her expectation that the therapist, because of the death of the fetus, would abandon their struggle for Jessica's life. Jessica feared that she was losing her own sense of existence, but the therapist's close attention to how the abortion had

reanimated critical pathogenic experiences slowly resto
strengthened her sense of herself.

When Jessica emerged from the crisis, she noticed that she
had not experienced any amnesia or depersonalization episodes
and was both pleased and somewhat disoriented by this change.
The therapist's upcoming weekend out of town was not anticipated by Jessica with her usual terror, because she "knew" the
therapist was coming back. She felt upset by the separation but
no longer believed that such a separation put her at the mercy of
her brother's awesome power. This transformation was understood by both the patient and therapist as an important developmental achievement in self-differentiation.

The fifth and final crisis of the treatment took place soon after
Jessica was beginning to feel a new sense of vitality and aliveness. She had recently been able to visit Justin's grave and feel
painfully saddened by his loss, although she was not yet completely free of the encumbering parental requirement that she be
Justin. Early one morning Jessica learned that her father, after
numerous dangerous climbing expeditions over the years, had
died following a bad fall down the side of a steep mountain.
Again her brother's "force" reared its ugly head, and she began
to feel that her existence was to blame for her father's death. She
felt hopeless about anything ever changing in her life, but again
she did not become suicidal. She did, however, experience intense anxiety, and she told the therapist that only their relationship provided the support that she needed to sustain herself. She
reported dreams in which she and the therapist were transported
back into her past, so that she could relive critical formative
experiences but with the protective presence of the therapist by
her side. The imagery of these dreams dramatized the extent to
which Jessica experienced the therapist as a new object firmly
aligned with her attempts to develop and nurture her own life
and demarcate herself from her brother.

After many months of therapeutic work, Jessica began to
remember certain crucial details related to Justin's illness—memories that, up to this point, had to be repressed because they
threatened the powerful parental requirement that she embody
Justin. The memories contradicted Jessica's belief that she had
indirectly caused Justin's death.

First, Jessica recalled that as a child she had often been told that Justin had been a very sickly little boy from birth, and she remembered that his vulnerability to illness had been well known in the family long before his enrollment in military school. She had "forgotten" this vital information and had imagined that he was healthy until contracting his fatal disease, in order to preserve the myth that she had caused his death by making it necessary for him to go away to military school. By maintaining her guilt and repressing any knowledge that challenged it, she complied with her parents' need for her to feel responsible for Justin and for preserving him within the fabric of her own being.

Second, in contrast to her parents' intense idealization of Justin during the last phase of his illness—an idealization with which she had felt required to comply—Jessica now came to remember him as a frightened, bitter adolescent boy struggling with the terrors of illness and impending death. She could now see that when Justin blamed her for his illness, this was the reaction of an angry and confused young boy, not a pronouncement from an all-knowing god.

The recovery of these memories helped Jessica to realize that her own continuing life had not been the cause of Justin's death. Indeed, despite her intense angry feelings toward him, she had loved him more than anyone else on earth. As her idealization of him subsided, along with the requirement that she preserve him within herself, she began a painful mourning process that had never been allowed before.

After much intensive therapeutic work, Jessica finally emerged from her delusional state, and, concomitantly, the depersonalization experiences disappeared, as did much of her self-destructive behavior. As the merger with Justin was broken, she expressed "burning desires" to have fun and to explore the possibilities of *her* life. This new-found sense of aliveness alternated with deep feelings of sadness and grief over the deaths of her brother and father. She had just begun to immerse herself in these feelings when she was accepted at a prestigious acting school in another part of the country. After a period of intense conflict, during which the multiple meanings of making such a move were carefully explored, she decided to accept the school's offer. On one hand, she was afraid that continuing to investigate her inner experience would pull her back into the merger with Justin, a danger from which she could flee by leaving treatment. On the other hand, her decision to leave reflected her considerable achievements in the area of self-differentiation, which enabled her to feel that she deserved to have a life centered on her own ambitions. She continued to contact the therapist from time to time, to reinstate their life-affirming bond. Three years after termination, she continued to be free of both the delusional merger and suicidality. While she is not without considerable inner strife and turmoil, her continuing existence seems assured.

DISCUSSION

The case of Jessica is a particularly clear example of derailment of the developmental process of self-differentiation – the evolving sense of being a distinct center of affective experience and personal agency, with individualized aims and goals. In an earlier work (Stolorow et al., 1987), it was proposed that specific, maturationally evolving selfobject experiences are necessary for facilitating, consolidating, expanding, and sustaining the development of differentiated selfhood during the entire life cycle. This developmental progression becomes disrupted when the requisite selfobject experiences needed to support the child's self-differentiating processes are absent or unsteady.

Derailment of the self-differentiation process occurs in an intersubjective situation in which central affect states associated with the development of individualized selfhood are consistently not responded to or are actively rejected. A fundamental psychic conflict thereby becomes enduringly established between the requirement that one's developmental course must conform to the emotional needs of caregivers and the inner imperative that its evolution be firmly rooted in a vitalizing affective core of one's own. As one of several possible outcomes of this basic conflict, the child may be compelled to abandon or severely compromise central affective strivings in order to maintain indispensable ties. As seen in the case of Jessica, this is the path of submission and chronic depression.

..t be recalled that a central theme in the transference in .ne early weeks of treatment was Jessica's belief that she had to mold herself to whatever the therapist needed her to be in order to maintain the therapeutic relationship. Moreover, Jessica experienced a profound sense of badness whenever she felt or did something that was not in harmony with what she thought the therapist required of her. Analysis of this transference paradigm produced a host of early memories in which the patient's mother would become injured, enraged, and attacking whenever her daughter's states of mind or behavior failed to conform to the mother's needs.

Other memories seemed to show quite clearly that the mother experienced attending to Jessica's emotional states and needs as an odious burden, particularly when Jessica was very small, and that her father was virtually unavailable as an alternate source of caregiving functions. Furthermore, her mother's many long absences, during which her contacts with Jessica were irregular and her return home unknown, left Jessica with a sense that her emotional importance to her mother was negligible and that the bond between them was quite tenuous. Jessica attempted to maintain this fragile tie by trying to be exactly the child her mother wished her to be, at the expense of her own affectivity and distinctness. Thus, Jessica's self-differentiating processes were already seriously compromised quite early in her relationship with her mother, establishing a pattern of self-subjugation and compliance with the requirements of others. It was with this preestablished organizing principle – self-surrender as the price for maintaining vital ties – that she entered the critical phase of her development ushered in by her brother's fatal illness. This invariant organizing principle set the stage for the pathological introjection that formed the basis of her chronic suicidality. When she perceived that her parents wanted her to incorporate and become Justin, she felt she had no choice but to comply and to sacrifice herself to their needs. Feeling that she was valueless and dispensable to her parents as the child she was (she had been essentially abandoned during the period of her brother's illness), she unconsciously hoped that by becoming Justin she would become as treasured by them as he seemed to be.

Historically, introjection has been explained as deriving from
the need to preserve a tie to an ambivalently loved lost object
(Freud, 1917). In this formulation, introjection is seen as a defense against a mourning process that cannot be tolerated because the feelings toward the lost object are too conflictual.
Certainly, Jessica's feelings toward her brother were ambiva-
lent–increasingly so during the period of his illness–and the
introjection did preserve the bond, alleviate her guilt over angry
wishes, and protect her from the pain of mourning. However,
while these defensive functions were not absent, they were not
of primary pathogenic significance. On the contrary, Jessica
longed to feel permitted to mourn the loss of her brother in order
to reclaim her own being, but this mourning process was *prohib-
ited* because it would violate her parents' requirement that she
keep him alive.

As we have stated, it is our view that an introject can be seen
as a region of invalidity in a person's experience that has been
filled in by the perceptions, judgments, feelings, or needs of
some emotionally significant other. If the validity of one's own
perceptual reality comes under unremitting attack, then this
experience of psychological usurpation may become increasingly dramatized and concretized until, ultimately, it reaches the
point of delusion. Such was the case with Jessica. Her parents
subjected her experience of her brother's illness and death to a
relentless regime of invalidation, to the point that she doubted
that he had died at all. In the same measure, their equally
relentless need to preserve him by seeing him in her profoundly
invalidated her experience of herself as a distinct person. The
resulting void in her subjective universe was filled by introjection. In compliance with her parents' need, she brought Justin to
life within herself, and, finally, she became he, virtually eradi-
cating her own existence.

The transference relationship that became heir to this history
of developmental derailment was, in broad brushstrokes, essentially bipolar in its organization (see Stolorow et al., 1987). At
one pole of the transference was Jessica's longing to experience
the therapist as a protective presence who would enable her to
reinstate self-differentiating processes that had been thwarted
during her formative years. In this dimension of the transfer-

ence, the patient hoped and searched for a new selfobject experience that would permit her to resume her arrested psychological development. At the other pole were her expectations and fears of a transference repetition of the original pathogenic experiences that had blocked the emergence of her own distinctness. This second dimension of the transference became a focal source of conflict and resistance in the therapy.

The course of treatment was characterized by continual shifts in the figure-ground relationships between these two poles of the transference, as they oscillated between the experiential foreground and background of the therapy. These oscillations were in large part determined by Jessica's perception of whether or not the therapist was firmly aligned with her struggle for self-delineation.

Early in the therapy, the repetitive dimension of the transference was preeminent. Jessica initially experienced the therapeutic relationship as very tenuous. She felt excluded from the therapist's "secret life" and doubted that she existed in the therapist's mind when not in her presence. She believed that she had to do and be whatever the therapist required in order to maintain the precarious tie between them. Any feeling that might have been out of harmony with, or a burden to, the therapist had to be sacrificed, for to bring such a feeling into the open would be to invite angry criticism, repulsion, and ultimate abandonment. The understanding and interpretation of these transference fears and expectations evoked much genetic material pertaining to the patient's early experiences with her mother and gradually mobilized Jessica's hope that she could have a different experience with the therapist.

As Jessica came to see the therapist as her only hope for survival as a distinct person, she experienced desperate yearnings for continuous union with her. Only when at one with the therapist could Jessica feel safe from the inner "force"–her brother–that threatened her with extinction. Early in the treatment, separations from the therapist or perceptions of any trace of dysphoria in the therapist's state of mind would abruptly obliterate this archaic selfobject transference experience and bring the repetitive aspect of the transference back into the foreground. When the therapist went away or seemed irritated, this meant to Jessica that the therapist must feel that she should be dead and would abandon her in her struggle to be free of Justin. Jessica's perception of the therapist at those times replicated her experience of her parents' demands that she sacrifice her own life to preserve Justin's.

Disturbances originating outside the therapeutic relationship could also disrupt the bond and strongly evoke the repetitive dimension of the transference. This was clearly seen in the first four of the five crises we have described, triggered respectively by the death of Jessica's boyfriend and the disappearance of her father, the anniversary of her brother's death, her enjoyment of her acting performance, and her abortion. Each of these crises evoked the familiar expectations in the transference that the therapist would see her as a murderer, feel she should be dead, and abandon the struggle for her life. In each instance, the therapist carefully explored these transference experiences with the patient and interpreted the invariant principles that organized them—the parental requirement that she sacrifice herself and the absolute prohibition against existing as a distinct person. The working through of each of these crises, and the analysis of the repetitive transference patterns that accompanied them, resulted, incrementally, in a gradual strengthening of the selfobject dimension of the transference. By the time of the death of her father, which precipitated the final crisis, the therapist had become firmly established for Jessica as a longed-for protector of her distinct selfhood. In the transference bond, she had found a facilitating matrix within which her aborted self-differentiating processes could safely be revitalized and her stalled development resumed.

It is clear that at termination the transference, in both its repetitive and selfobject dimensions, had not been fully worked through or transformed. Jessica continued to need occasional brief contacts with the therapist to sustain her. However, significant structural reorganization had been achieved. Partially liberated from the grip of the requirement that she incorporate and be her brother, she could now experience and affirm her own distinctness and affective vitality without feeling herself to be an omnipotent destroyer. She felt a new freedom to embrace life with enthusiasm, and her chronic suicidality had disappeared.

II

Clinical Applications

Chapter 6

Varieties of Therapeutic Alliance

(written in collaboration with Bernard Brandchaft)

FEW WOULD DISPUTE THAT THE ESTABLISHMENT of a bond between analyst and patient that permits the work of analysis to unfold is a sine qua non of our work. Yet serious differences exist regarding the essential nature of this bond, and the clinical implications of these differences are profound. The problem of resistances has thwarted psychoanalysts in their efforts to bring about more predictable structural change and led to the establishment of criteria for analyzability that increasingly exclude large numbers of persons seeking analysis (Waelder, 1960; Greenson, 1967). Freud's (1937) final work, "Analysis Terminable and Interminable," reflected his preoccupation with the severe limitations posed by resistances on the therapeutic efficacy of psychoanalysis. In this summary he held a large number of factors, all intrapsychic, to account. If Freud's conclusions were to be accepted as final, psychoanalysts would be faced with either an analytic procedure severely restricted in its scope or the necessity of having to alter significantly the basic principles and techniques of psychoanalysis in the hope of increasing its therapeutic effectiveness. This dilemma provided a powerful stimulus for the reexamination of the nature of the therapeutic bond. And so the concept of a therapeutic alliance, already implicit in much of Freud's writings, became the focus of great interest in the 1950s.

In retrospect, it is clear that in the United States the interest in the therapeutic alliance, a particular object relationship between patient and analyst (Sterba, 1934; Bibring, 1937; Fenichel, 1941; Greenson, 1954; Zetzel, 1956; Stone, 1961), was stimulated by the development of ego psychology and paralleled the burgeoning interest in the more general subject of object relations in Great Britain, as exemplified in the work of Klein, as well as that of Winnicott, Balint, and Fairbairn. Both developments were rooted in the recognition that breakdowns of the therapeutic process come about because of disruptions within the analytic dyad, and so it was to these subjects that analysts turned their attention in attempts to extend the scope of analytic influence.

The ego psychologists, focusing on the central role of the ego in development and pathogenesis, visualized the analytic relationship as having two dimensions. One was rooted in the patient's identification with the analyst and especially with his understanding of the patient's unconscious. This, they held, was the basis for the therapeutic alliance. The other part of the patient's ego was engaged in resistance to the unfolding of the unconscious regressive instinctual forces and the structural conflicts that constituted the pathogenic oedipal complex of the transference neurosis. The maintenance of the therapeutic alliance was dependent on bringing about a split between an experiencing ego and a more reasonable, detached, and observing ego (Zetzel, 1956; Greenson, 1967) in order to deal with the resistance. This was to be facilitated by the patient's rational wish to cooperate with the analyst in order to overcome his suffering and by "his ability to follow the instructions and insights of the analyst" (Greenson, 1967, p. 192). Greenson emphasized the patient's identification with the analyst's interpretive approach as the specific goal of the therapeutic alliance. He took a step away from the traditional view when he considered the establishment of this relationship between patient and analyst, the "ingredient which is vital for the success or failure of psychoanalytic treatment," as "relatively nonneurotic, rational"—in other words, *nontransference* (p. 46).

It is to be emphasized that in describing the establishment of a therapeutic alliance the ego psychologists were claiming not only that the patient must identify with the analyst's basic investigative methods and with such general principles as transference, resistance, and unconscious forces shaping subjective experience. The process of identification also had to include the analyst's theory-rooted assumptions about the patient's basic motivations and about the contents of the patient's mind. Thus, if the patient rejected or failed to recognize the correctness of the analyst's view that drive-related conflicts, particularly the oedipal conflict, were central in his symptoms and in his development, this continued to be regarded as the ultimate expression of the rivalry belonging to the very oedipal complex that the analyst had been seeking to uncover, now inevitably working its way into the transference (Abraham, 1919).

Understanding the resistance as deriving from conflicts arising solely from within the patient, the ego psychologists also required the patient to identify with the analyst's view of himself as essentially neutral in relation to the patient's conflicts, a blank screen upon which these were played out. Accordingly, transference was to be seen as the result of the patient's displacements or distortions, except where it might be influenced by those countertransference intrusions that the analyst was able to recognize. Chronic and intractable resistances were believed to be signs of negative therapeutic reactions or unanalyzability and were ascribed to ego weakness or a masochistic need to fail.

The dominant school of object relations in Great Britain, that of Melanie Klein, on the other hand, held that the therapeutic alliance was embedded in the transference, which itself was a complex object relation. The attachment of a "normal" dependent part of the self to a "good" part-object, the breast, was revived in the analysis, and the identification with it formed the nucleus of the therapeutic alliance. Disruptions in this bond were attributed to the operation of primitive defensive measures of the ego, which shaped and distorted the patient's perception of "real objects," including the analyst, and resulted in pathogenic introjections of cruel objects or objects damaged in omnipotent fantasy by the patient's destructiveness. The reestablishment of the therapeutic bond, and with it a secure tie with good, protecting, and protected internal objects, was thought to be the foundation of growth and creativity. This was brought about by the interpretation of the unconscious archaic defense mechanisms, by the working through of the infantile conflicts of ambivalence and pathological envy that the patient was defending against, and by the patient's developing trust in the analyst and his explanations of the nature of the patient's subjective experience, anxieties, and depressive feelings.

Klein (1950), unlike the ego psychologists, believed that the functioning of the ego was at all times determined by its relationships to its external and internal objects. Archaic ties between the ego and primitive objects or part-objects existed from the beginning, she insisted, and thus the history of any individual's development could be found in the record of the complex relationship between ego and objects. As a consequence of this view, the scope of psychoanalysis was for her automatically extended. The constitutional strengths or adaptability of the patient's ego were not stressed as a prerequisite, and consequently, children and psychotics were accepted, in principle, as being suitable for analysis. This remained a point of contention between the two schools.

Strachey's (1934) conceptualization of the "mutative interpretation" illustrates the Kleinian view of the therapeutic process. Strachey believed, as did the ego psychologists, that identification with the analyst occupied a central role. For him the operative mechanism was that of introjection, whereby the analyst's interpretations enabled him to be installed as a less severe and more benign influence than the patient's existing internal objects or superego. However, in Strachey's formulation the mutative value of the object relation to the analyst lay not only in an analytic attitude or stance that might open the possibility of a transforming introjection. It was essential that the identificatory process extend to the analyst's interpretations of the impulses and defenses that characterize the paranoid-schizoid and depressive positions postulated by Klein, since these were assumed to reappear in the transference. These "mutative interpretations" would have to be accepted as "true," so that the patient's view of himself and his history would come to conform to what the analyst had reflected to him.

Her followers adhered to a stance whose basic principles Klein (1961) described as follows:

The psychoanalytic procedure consists in selecting the most urgent aspects of the material and interpreting them with precision. *The patient's reactions and subsequent associations amount to further material which has to be analyzed in the same way* . . . I was determined not to modify my technique and to interpret in the usual way even deep anxiety situations as they came up and the corresponding defenses [pp. 12–13; emphasis added].

The interpretive principles derive from Klein's view of the central importance of primitive defense mechanisms, especially splitting and projective identification, directed against internal instinctual forces or internal objects distorted by projected contents. Within this system intense and prolonged resistances leading to negative therapeutic reactions were and continue to be ascribed to the workings of pathological destructive envy, a vicissitude of the death instinct (Klein, 1957; Joseph, 1982; Rosenfeld, 1987). This clinical formulation is hardly surprising in view of the primary etiologic role Klein's metapsychology attributed to the innate conflict between life and death instincts. Here also, as in the case of the ego psychologists, the unsuccessful therapeutic result was assumed to demonstrate the correctness of the theory no less than the successful one. Despite their profound differences, in this crucial aspect these two divergent theoretical schools were in accord. The therapeutic alliance and the success of the analysis were held to depend on the ability of the patient ultimately to see the events of the analysis according to the basic concepts that organized and informed the analyst's observations and interpretations. This is a requirement with which patients often felt compelled to comply as the price for maintaining the vitally needed tie to the analyst.

We have chosen to discuss the concepts and practices of these two dominant schools not only because of their leading position and continuing influence on psychoanalytic thought, but also because, in their approach to the therapeutic bond, they illustrate a basic and largely unchallenged philosophical assumption that has pervaded psychoanalytic thought since its inception, namely, the existence of an "objective reality" that is known by the analyst and distorted by the patient (Atwood and Stolorow, 1984; Stolorow, Brandchaft, and Atwood, 1987). This assumption lies at the heart of the traditional view of transference and its insistence on the dichotomy between the patient's experience of the analyst as distortion and the analyst's experience of himself as real. This dichotomy is one of the foundation stones on which the more elaborate and experience-distant theoretical scaffoldings of the two divergent psychoanalytic schools have been built. It is not the philosophical assumption with which we are here concerned, but the serious and insufficiently acknowledged consequences of its clinical application.

In agreement with Schwaber (1983), we contend that the only reality relevant and accessible to psychoanalytic inquiry (that is, to empathy and introspection) is *subjective reality*—that of the patient, that of the analyst, and the psychological field created by the interplay between the two. The belief that one's personal reality is objective is an instance of the psychological process of concretization, the symbolic transformation of *configurations of subjective experience* into events and entities that are believed to be *objectively* perceived and known (Atwood and Stolorow, 1984). Attributions of objective reality, in other words, are concretizations of subjective truth. As we have observed this process in ourselves and others, we have become aware that it operates automatically and prereflectively.

Adherence to the doctrine of objective reality and its corollary concept of distortion has led both psychoanalytic schools to view pathology in terms of processes and mechanisms located solely within the patient. This emphasis blinds the clinician to the impact of the observer on the observed as an intrinsic, ever-present factor in the psychoanalytic situation, and it obscures the profound ways in which the analyst himself and his theories are implicated in the phenomena he observes and seeks to treat. When the concept of distortion is imposed, a *cordon sanitaire* is established, which forecloses the investigation of the analyst's contribution in depth. The invitation that the patient identify with the analyst's concepts as a condition for a therapeutic alliance is an invitation to cure by compliance. Alternatively, it can trigger the appearance of what seems to be a resistance. Investigation of the patient's experience may reveal, however, an important attempt at self-differentiation, an attempt to protect an independent center of perception and affectivity from usurpation. When the patient reacts adversely to the analyst's explanations, the idea that these disruptive reactions arise from purely intrapsychic causes and are to be explained by the same concepts that are producing the reactions sets the stage for those chronic disjunctions that have been described as negative transference resistances or negative therapeutic reactions (Brandchaft, 1983; Atwood and Stolorow, 1984). When analysts invoke the concept of objective reality along with its corollary concept of distortion, this forecloses and diverts the investigation of the subjective reality encoded in the patient's communications, a reality that is precisely what the psychoanalytic method is uniquely equipped to illuminate.

What, from our intersubjective perspective, constitutes the essence of a therapeutic alliance? It is surely not the bond formed by the patient's commitment to follow the insights of the analyst. In our view the foundations of a therapeutic alliance are established by the analyst's commitment to seek consistently to comprehend the meaning of the patient's expressions, his affect states, and, most centrally, the impact of the analyst from a perspective *within* rather than outside the patient's subjective frame of reference (Kohut, 1959). We have referred to this positioning as the stance of "sustained empathic inquiry." Let no one believe that this commitment is an easy one to fulfill – it is frequently like feeling the sand giving way under one's psychological footing. Seeing himself and the world consistently through the eyes of another can pose serious threats to the analyst's personal reality and sense of self, much as the patient must feel threatened when his experience is treated as a distortion of reality.

What are the advantages of this stance? It opens for further psychoanalytic illumination those disruptions of the analytic bond that produce stubborn resistances that threaten to become entrenched. Disjunctions arising from frustration, disappointment, and experiences of misattunement are the inevitable consequence of the profoundly intersubjective nature of the analytic dialogue, the colliding of differently organized subjective galaxies. They are *not* to be regarded as errors in an "objective" sense. They are, however, evidence that the impact of the analyst and his understanding, or lack thereof, is central to the patient's subjective reality, and thus they provide access to crucial areas of the patient's inner world. The commitment to extend empathic inquiry to these experiences of disruption and to view them from within the patient's subjective framework, with the observer as an immanent part of the experience, repeatedly reestablishes and mends the therapeutic bond. Access is then provided to the specific and idiosyncratic ways in which the patient is organizing his experience of the analyst and to the meanings that this experience has come to encode. A window is thrown open for a fresh look into the area of discrepant and conflictful experience, into a room in which are locked the most intimate of secrets and longings and the most personal of happenings. It is from this space that a "new beginning" may take root.

What are the goals that join the participants in the therapeutic alliance? They are the progressive unfolding, illumination, and transformation of the patient's subjective universe. When the analyst and the patient are freed of the need to justify their respective realities, the process of self-reflection is encouraged and vitalized for both. Inevitably, it emerges that the central motivational configurations mobilized in analysis are derailed developmental strivings, and the course of the developmental processes activated by the analysis becomes the focus of inquiry. The experiences of vitality and devitalization, of buoyant aliveness and apathy, which are clues to the unfolding developmental processes and their derailment, can be followed, while the effect of the analyst as he is experienced in this ebb and flow is always kept in view.

It cannot be emphasized too strongly that the analyst's acceptance of the validity of the patient's perceptual reality in the ongoing delineation of intrapsychic experience is of inestimable importance in establishing the therapeutic alliance. Any threat to the validity of perceptual reality constitutes a deadly threat to the self and to the organization of experience itself. When the analyst insists that the patient's perception is a secondary phenomenon distorted by primary forces, this, more than any other single factor, ushers in the conflictful transference-countertransference spirals that are so commonly described as resistances to analysis or negative transferences. These can be recognized as crises or impasses in which each partner in the erstwhile therapeutic alliance becomes engaged in desperately attempting to maintain his own organization of experience against the threat to it posed by the other. Schwaber (1984) has also pointed out that many of our patients suffer from a primary sense of uncertainty about the reality of inner experience. For them the recognition and articulation of vaguely felt affect states or perceptions is especially meaningful (p. 161). For others the development of the ability to sustain a belief in their own subjective reality was derailed because their perceptions contained information that was threatening to caregivers. The perceptions thereby became the source of continuing conflict and had to be repudiated. This familiar core experience has been dramatized in the "gaslight" genre. We have presented three cases (Stolorow et al., 1987) in which the inability to maintain one's own perceptual reality appeared to be a factor predisposing to psychotic states. In these cases delusion formation represented a desperate attempt to substantialize and preserve a perceptual reality that had come under assault and begun to crumble. We stressed particularly the noxious role unwittingly played in therapeutic situations by failures of the analyst to recognize the core of subjective truth encoded in the patient's communications.

The specific attunement to "the role of the analyst and of the surround, as perceived and experienced by the patient . . . as intrinsic to [his] reality . . . draws upon modalities which are significant components of the essentials of parental empathy—attunement to and recognition of the perceptions and experiential states of another" (Schwaber, 1984, p. 160). In the transference such attunement is a constituent of a quintessential self-delineating experience serving to reinstate aborted developmental processes of articulating and consolidating subjective reality. No more active mirroring is ordinarily required than the analyst's continuing, active interest in, and acceptance of, the perceptual validity of his patient's experience, together with his alertness to cues of disavowed affect states that signal perceptions the patient cannot as yet admit into his subjective world.

The stance of sustained empathic inquiry consolidates the therapeutic alliance as it enhances and extends the domain of safety and harmony within the intersubjective field. The continuing articulation and consolidation of subjective reality is, however, only a part of the therapeutic experience. The additional goal of the therapeutic alliance is the transformation of subjective experience. We will not focus here on the transformational prospects for the analyst in discovering his impact and that of his inferences on the patient or in reflecting on the invariant principles that organize his experience of himself and his patient. Instead we wish to emphasize that a milieu in which the patient's perceptual reality is not threatened encourages the patient to develop and expand his own capacity for self-reflection. Access is thereby gained into unfolding patterns of experience reflecting structural weakness, psychological constriction, early developmental derailment, and archaic defensive activity—that is, the specific patterns that await transformation.

Often analysts fear that the commitment to understanding from within the patient's own subjective framework, and especially to recognizing and investigating the analyst's contribution to the patient's experience, will result in an obfuscation of the patient's contribution to his own circumstances. We find this fear to be unwarranted. Central to the process of transformation is the understanding of the ways in which the patient's experience of the analytic dialogue is *codetermined* throughout by the organizing activities of *both* participants. The patient's unconscious structuring activity is discernible in the distinctively personal *meanings* that the analyst's activities—and especially his interpretive activity—repeatedly and invariantly come to acquire for the patient.

We have often heard critics voice an erroneous impression that the domain of empathic inquiry extends only to conscious elements of subjective experience. On the contrary, an indispensable part of the work of analysis involves the investigation of how conscious experience is organized according to hierarchies of unconscious principles. These determine the ways in which the patient's experiences are recurrently patterned according to developmentally preformed themes and meanings. It is in the illumination of these meanings, and of the subjective truths they encode, that the therapeutic alliance and psychoanalysis itself finds its most generative purpose.

Consider, for example, the difficulties regularly encountered when attempting to treat patients whose severe developmental deprivations have predisposed them to intense distrust, violent affective reactions, or stubborn defensiveness. In such patients we have become aware of underlying unconscious and invariant organizing principles into which all experience tends to be assimilated. From their early history has crystalized a certain conviction that nothing good could happen to them in relation to another person, that no one could possibly care for them, that they are doomed ultimately to live and die alone, and that any hope for a meaningful life based on an inner design of their own is an illusion and a certain invitation to disaster. Every experience of disappointment or limitation tends to confirm one or another of these principles. The impact of such experiences is not felt to be delimited and temporary, but global and eternal. Consequently, such inevitable experiences lead inexorably to resignation and walling off or to violent affective reactions. The subsequent trajectory of self-experience is codetermined both by the impact of external events and by the invariant ordering principles into which these events are assimilated and from which they derive their meaning.

We are not unmindful of certain dangers posed by the therapeutic alliance as we have conceptualized it. When the stance of empathic inquiry, for example, facilitates the appearance of archaic longings expressed in concrete demands to occupy a special place or to be given special consideration, there is a tendency for the analyst to be catapulted into a concreteness of his own and to react in either of two ways. On one hand, reacting defensively, he may insist that his patient recognize the unrealistic nature of these demands. On the other hand, he may react from a feeling of responsibility for the patient's disappointment and give covert encouragement to the patient's underlying hope for a relationship purified of any repetition of childhood traumata. Either course diminishes the likelihood of thoroughgoing change through the transformation of existing structures. Only the consistent working through in the analysis of the developmentally determined, invariant organizing principles can achieve the structural change so hopefully envisioned by the pioneers of our calling.

To illustrate our view of the therapeutic alliance, we offer some critical commentary on a case report by a well-known and respected psychoanalytic clinician and theoretician. Kernberg (1987) writes of a woman who "started her psychoanalysis suffering from a hysterical personality, consistent inhibition of orgasm in intercourse with her husband, and romantic attachments in fantasy to unavailable men" (p. 802). After the patient, with the help of the analyst, had overcome her reluctance to speak about her fears of him, she expressed the fantasy that he "was particularly sensual, in fact, 'lecherous,' and might be attempting to arouse her sexual feelings . . . so as to obtain sexual gratification from her" (p. 802). She said that the basis for her fears was that she had heard he came from a Latin American country and had written about erotic love relations. Furthermore, the analyst writes,

> She thought I had a particularly seductive attitude toward the women working in the office area where I saw her. All this, she considered, *justified* her fears. She expressed the fantasy that I was looking at her in peculiar ways as she came to sessions, and that I probably was trying to guess the shape of her body underneath her clothes as she lay on the couch [p. 802, emphasis added].

Her attitude was not seductive. On the contrary, she was "inhibited, rigid, almost asexual in her behavior" (p. 802), and there was very little eroticism in her nonverbal communications. The analyst took notice of all this and noticed also, on reflection, that his own emotional reactions and fantasies about her had a subdued quality and contained no conscious erotic element. On the basis of these observations he concluded "that she was attributing to me her own repressed sexual fantasies and wishes" and that "this typical example of a neurotic transference illustrates the operation of projection,[1] with little activation of

---

[1]The assumption that transference experiences are to be explained by the operation of defensive measures is undoubtedly shared by a majority of analysts. It is precisely for this reason that we are urging a reexamination of the clinical evidence. We wish to emphasize that it is not the particular theory-rooted content of Kernberg's interpretations that we are questioning here. What we are calling into question is the *epistemological stance* according to which the analyst, through his acts of self-reflection, is presumed to have

countertransference material either in a broad . . . or in the restricted sense" (p. 802).

The report goes on to describe changes that took place during the ensuing year. The patient's fear of the analyst's sexual interest in her was succeeded by expressions of her disgust for the sexual interest older men have for younger women, and she discovered features of her father in these lecherous old men. Her own romantic fantasies, meanwhile, remained fixed on unavailable men, while she was terrified of sexual engagements with men, including her husband, who were available to her. As she became aware, the analyst writes, that her sexual excitement was associated with forbidden sexual relations, there was a decrease in her "repression and projection of sexual feelings in the transference" (p. 803). She stopped feeling that the analyst was interested in her sexually and, as he had anticipated and interpreted from the beginning, she began to have "direct oedipal" sexual fantasies about him.

At one point, in response to her fantasies, the analyst found himself responding erotically and with a fantasy of his own that he in turn would enjoy a sexual relation with her, "breaking all conventional barriers" and providing her "with a gift of the fullest acknowledgment of her specialness and attractiveness" (p. 803). The analyst describes this as a transitory emotional response to her seduction in the transference, which had activated in him "the complementary attitude of a fantasied, seductive oedipal father" (p. 803). Subsequently the patient once more accused the analyst of teasing and humiliating her and, finding no indication of what the patient perceived, the analyst concluded that the patient was projecting onto him experiences with her father from the past.

In this latter series of associations and interpretations, as in the others cited, there is no indication of an attempt to explore fully

---

gained privileged access to the objective truth about himself that the patient's discrepant perceptions are then said to distort. This stance does not have to be inferred from Kernberg's clinical material; it is readily demonstrated in his descriptions of how he arrived at transference interpretations. Our growing awareness of the unintended and unexamined impact of this epistemological stance on the course of the therapeutic process was one of the central concerns that motivated us to write this chapter.

the *basis* of the patient's experience from within the perspective of her own subjective frame of reference. Perhaps she perceived something in his tone or his manner that he had not intended or even been aware of. Did his initial scrutiny of her for signs of "eroticism" mean something else for her? Did his fantasy of a sexual affair with her, which he believed was reactive, communicate itself to her in some way and stimulate concerns in her? The point here is not that the analyst "objectively" did anything wrong; he clearly kept well within the boundaries of professional behavior. The point is that whatever singular meanings these or other cues from the analyst might have had for the patient are left unexplored. Only what conformed to the theory being employed was attended to. The analyst in this case used as primary data his own self-reflections, and these persuaded him that the patient's experience was the consequence of distorting mechanisms. Here the analyst's subjective frame of reference is elevated to the status of objective fact; and the patient must accept the analyst's view as objective, as part of the working alliance. Otherwise, as the report describes, the resistance has to be worked through so that she can come to recognize her defenses against accepting the analyst's perceptions, presumably because she is afraid to face her own impulses. One reality, the analyst's, is apparently real; the other, the patient's, is false! The therapeutic task is to account for the "distortion."

However, a crucial source of data is left unexplored. Access to that source, that is, an investigation in depth of the elements of the patient's experience from within *her* subjective framework, is bypassed when the stance of empathic inquiry is abandoned in favor of doctrinal inference. A process is derailed that might have disclosed how seduction was being signaled for *this* patient. Acceptance of the perceptual (not objective) validity of the patient's experience might have made possible a therapeutic alliance committed to an investigation of the exquisitely personal meanings of seduction and humiliation into which the various cues from the side of the analyst were being assimilated.

It is also possible that such investigation might have provided a safer milieu wherein elements of the patient's experience of her husband that would have illuminated her aversion to his sexual advances could have been articulated. Her extramarital sexual fantasies might then have disclosed, not an oedipal fixation, but sequestered hopes for acceptance, responsiveness, and enrichment not otherwise available to her.

The patient, it is reported, gradually came to realize her defenses against her sexual feelings and produced oedipal wishes toward the analyst. Such expressions are commonly taken as proof of the correctness of the theory of drive and defense. However, nothing illustrates more clearly the need for the analyst to investigate from within the patient's subjective framework the impact of his own theories on the direction and course of the analysis. In the establishment of a therapeutic alliance, *two heads are surely better than one.* Only this can enable patient and analyst to distinguish between a "pseudoalliance" based on compliance with the analyst's viewpoint and a therapeutically mutative alliance based on empathic inquiry into the patient's subjective world.

There is more than an echo here of the quandary Freud encountered that changed the whole course of the evolution of psychoanalysis. Freud found evidence that some of the childhood sexual seductions his patients complained of could not have happened and, it is reported, he felt betrayed. He concluded that these must have been fantasies that expressed the childhood wishes of his female patients, and he built his subsequent theories of psychosexual development and of transference on that foundation. For Freud these fantasies were mental representations of instincts. However, sustained empathic inquiry reveals that such fantasies often encode experiences of traumatic developmental derailment and that Freud's dilemma was a false one. It is common for experiences of abuse and seduction of a nonsexual or covertly sexual nature to be concretized and preserved in sexual symbolism. This insight into the kernel of truth encoded in a patient's fantasies opens up a whole new pathway for exploration, one that remains foreclosed when a patient's perceptions are dismissed as distortion.

CONCLUSIONS

We have offered a critique of the concept of the therapeutic alliance implicit in both traditional ego psychology and Kleinian psychoanalysis. Specifically, we have objected to the notion that the therapeutic alliance requires that the patient identify not only with the analyst's analytic stance of empathic inquiry, but also with his theoretical presuppositions as well. We hold that such an alliance is actually a form of transference compliance, which the patient may believe is necessary in order to maintain the therapeutic bond on which all hopes for his future have come to depend. We have contrasted this "pseudoalliance" with a therapeutic alliance established through sustained empathic inquiry into the patient's subjective world. This latter alliance, in which the perceptual validity of the patient's transference experience is accepted, promotes the illumination and transformation of the invariant principles that unconsciously organize the patient's inner life. Material from a recently published case report is examined in order to illustrate the differing clinical consequences of fostering one or another of these two varieties of therapeutic alliance.

We are aware that analysts of all persuasions approach their patients with preconceived ideas and that any theoretical framework, including our own, can be perceived by patients as something with which they must compliantly identify. What we are emphasizing is that the commitment to investigating the impact of the analyst, of his interpretive activity, and of his theoretical preconceptions, whatever they may be, from within the perspective of the patient's own subjective reality is central to the establishment of a therapeutic context in which the patient's unconscious organizing principles can be most sharply illuminated and thereby become accessible to therapeutic transformation.

Chapter 7

Varieties of Therapeutic Impasse

(written in collaboration with Jeffrey L. Trop)

OUR THESIS IN THIS CHAPTER IS THAT IMPASSES in psychoanalytic therapy, when investigated from the standpoint of the principles unconsciously organizing the experiences of patient and therapist, provide a unique pathway – a "royal road" – to the attainment of psychoanalytic understanding.

From the continual interplay between the patient's and the therapist's psychological worlds two basic situations repeatedly arise: *intersubjective conjunction* and *intersubjective disjunction.* The first of these is illustrated by instances in which the principles structuring the patient's experiences give rise to expressions that are assimilated into closely similar central configurations in the psychological life of the therapist. Disjunction, by contrast, occurs when the therapist assimilates the material expressed by the patient into configurations that significantly alter its meaning for the patient. Repetitive occurrences of intersubjective conjunction and disjunction are inevitable accompaniments of the therapeutic process and reflect the interaction of differently organized subjective worlds.

Whether these intersubjective situations facilitate or obstruct the progress of therapy depends in large part on the extent of the therapist's ability to become reflectively aware of the organizing principles of his own subjective world. When such reflective self-awareness on the part of the therapist is reliably present, then the correspondence or disparity between the subjective worlds of patient and therapist can be used to promote empathic understanding and insight. In the case of an intersubjective conjunction that has been recognized, for example, the therapist may be able to find in his own life analogues of the experiences presented to him, his self-knowledge thus serving as an invaluable adjunct source of information regarding the probable background meanings of the patient's expressions. Disjunctions, once they are recognized, may also assist the therapist's ongoing efforts to understand the patient, for then his own emotional reactions can serve as potential intersubjective indices of the configurations actually structuring the patient's experiences.

In the absence of reflective self-awareness on the part of the therapist, such conjunctions and disjunctions can seriously impede the progress of therapy. For example, an intersubjective conjunction may interfere with the course of treatment when the patient's experiences so closely correspond to those of the therapist that they are not recognized as containing psychologically significant material to be investigated and understood. Descriptions of the patient's life that are in agreement with the therapist's personal vision of the world will accordingly tend to be regarded as reflections of objective reality rather than as manifestations of the patient's personality. Commonly, the specific region of intersubjective correspondence that escapes analytic inquiry reflects a defensive solution shared by both patient and therapist. The conjunction results in a mutual strengthening of resistance and counter-resistance and, hence, in a prolongation of the treatment.

The Case of Peter

Peter (whose treatment was discussed in Atwood and Stolorow, 1984), repeatedly complained about the mechanization and depersonalization of American life and expressed longings for a Utopian community within which his existence could have significance and meaning. His therapist, who shared this negative image of our society, never responded analytically to these expressions, for they seemed to him nothing more than indicants of good reality-testing regarding the modern condition of life. Both of them were prone to attribute the difficulties in their relationships to impersonal forces and institutions, and moreover to longing for a world modeled on the idealized images of vanished past eras in their respective lives. The preoccupation with these images also served to prevent a painful confrontation with certain conflictual issues concerning intimacy and attachment. The conjunction between patient and therapist here extended not only to the content of the expressed imagery, but also to aspects of its defensive purpose. The opportunity to illuminate the meanings and sources of the material, which also contained implications for the transference, was thus replaced by an unwitting, silent collusion to limit the patient's (and therapist's) attainment of self-knowledge.

NEGATIVE THERAPEUTIC REACTIONS

Especially damaging are the interferences with treatment that arise in consequence of protracted, unrecognized intersubjective disjunctions. In such instances, the disparity between patient and therapist can contribute to the formation of vicious countertherapeutic spirals that produce for each an ever more dramatic confrontation with dreaded scenes having salience in their respective subjective lives. Such persistent disjunctions, whereby empathy is chronically replaced by misunderstanding, invariably intensify and exacerbate the patient's suffering and manifest psychopathology. It is here that we find the source of what analysts have euphemistically termed "negative therapeutic reactions."

The concept of a "negative therapeutic reaction" was created by analysts to explain those disquieting situations in which interpretations that were presumed to be correct actually make patients worse rather than better. Typically, such untoward reactions to the analyst's well-intended interpretive efforts are attributed exclusively to intrapsychic mechanisms located entirely within the patient, such as an unconscious sense of guilt and a need for punishment, primal masochism (Freud, 1923, 1937), narcissistic character resistances (Abraham, 1919), a need to ward off the depressive position through omnipotent control (Riviere, 1936), or unconscious envy and a resulting compulsion to spoil the analytic work (Kernberg, 1975; Klein, 1957). We are contending, by contrast, that such therapeutic impasses and disasters cannot be understood apart from the intersubjective contexts in which they arise.

In our experience, exacerbations and entrenchments of patients' psychopathology severe enough to be termed "negative therapeutic reactions" are most often produced by prolonged, unrecognized intersubjective disjunctions wherein the patient's emotional needs are consistently misunderstood and thereby relentlessly rejected by the therapist. Such misunderstandings typically take the form of erroneously interpreting the revival of an unmet developmental longing as if it were an expression of malignant, pathological resistance. When the patient revives such a longing within the therapeutic relationship, and the therapist repeatedly interprets this developmental necessity as if it were merely a pathological resistance, the patient will experience such misinterpretations as gross failures of attunement. Consequently, traumatic psychological injuries are repeatedly inflicted, with impact similar to the pathogenic events of the patient's early life (Kohut, 1971; Stolorow and Lachmann, 1980).

The Case of Robyn

An example of such a destructive turn of events is found in the treatment of Robyn (discussed in Atwood and Stolorow, 1984), a woman whose difficulties traced back to her early family's consistent failure to provide the confirming and validating responsiveness necessary for the formation of a stable and coherent sense of self. The only exception to this pattern of unresponsiveness that she could recall was her father's sexual interest in her, which, according to her memories began when she was nine years old. She subsequently developed a seductive and coquettish style and ultimately a pattern of compulsive promiscuity with father-surrogates, in a desperate effort to be recognized and counteract terrible feelings of depletion and nonbeing.

Robyn's therapist began her treatment in accord with his understanding of the precepts of classical psychoanalysis, which included such an overly literal interpretation of the rule of abstinence that he responded to her urgent requests for affirming, mirroring responses with silence or at most a brief interpretation. She began to experience his seeming aloofness and "neutrality" as a repetition of the traumatically depriving circumstances of her childhood and alternated in treatment between sexualization of the transference and attempted seductions, on one hand, and expressions of deep rage on the other.

A central configuration in the therapist's subjective world concerned issues of power and control. The salience of these issues had largely arisen from a problematic childhood relationship with his mother, in which he had violently resisted submitting to what he felt was her tyrannizing and oppressive will. The dilemma around which major aspects of his subjective life were organized was the danger of relinquishing control and autonomy, which seemed to him equivalent to becoming the slavelike extension of others. The patient's desperate demands for mirroring responsiveness were unconsciously assimilated into his emotionally charged themes of power and control, evoking a reaction of stubborn resistance and entrenching his already withholding and unresponsive style. Unaware of the countertransference reaction that had been precipitated, he envisioned his patient's intensifying demands as expressive of a malignant need for dominance. A vicious spiral was thereby created, in which the disjunctive perceptions, needs, and reactions of patient and therapist strengthened one another in a reciprocally destructive way. The treatment continued in this situation for 18 months until it was finally broken off when the patient attempted to commit suicide.

IMPASSES: A ROYAL ROAD

Having reviewed and illustrated the kinds of intersubjective situations that, when not recognized, can lead to serious obstructions of the therapeutic process, we turn now to the central focus of this chapter—the new understandings and enhancements of the therapeutic process that can be achieved when the principles unconsciously organizing the experiences of patient and therapist in an impasse are successfully investigated and illuminated.

The Case of Alice

Alice was a 34-year-old teacher of Oriental descent who had entered therapy two years prior to the impasse to be described because she felt depressed about a relationship she was having with an older man whom she had been seeing for a year. She felt that this man had become more interested in his own activities than in her and was not attending to her needs. In particular, she felt he had been ignoring her when she wanted attention and physical affection. She appeared as an attractive and well-dressed woman whose quiet manner often betrayed her agitated state of mind.

She had been married in her early 20s for about a year, but the marriage ended when her husband began to withdraw from her and she became increasingly rageful with him. She had no children, a lack that continued to be a disappointment to her, and she experienced a chronic sense of loss, along with a persistent feeling that she was not feminine and that she was a failure as a woman. She was able to put these feelings aside only when she was working, and she described how happy she was teaching her students about reading and history. She often imagined that they were her children and thereby achieved an illusory sense of completeness.

Alice described a longstanding inner experience of deficiency and lack of confidence in her attractiveness. She was an only child, born when her parents were quite old. Consistent with his cultural background, her father had desperately wanted a male child. Throughout her childhood her mother and other relatives had told her repeatedly about his disappointment when she was born. Apparently he had become convinced that, because his wife was having a child late in their marriage, the child was destined to be the boy he had always wanted. He was devastated when she was born, and he precipitously left the family for several months. When he returned, and continuing throughout her childhood, he virtually ignored her and had little to do with her, leaving her care entirely to her mother. The patient emphasized to the therapist that her father had never been overtly cruel to her, but that it felt to her as if she did not really exist in his eyes. He seemed completely absorbed in his professional work, and she believed he regarded her as an obstacle to his ambitions. He remained distant and uninvolved with her until his sudden death when she was 16 years old.

Her mother was a very critical and perfectionistic woman who often seemed overwhelmed by her household tasks. Her mother had told her several times about her father's reactions to her birth without showing much emotion, but the patient had a persistent impression that her mother, too, had felt ashamed because Alice was not a boy. Her mother did encourage the patient's love of books, and the patient became more and more withdrawn growing up, retreating into the world of literature and fantasy. She was very shy and isolated during her childhood but distinguished herself academically and decided to go into teaching.

As she described her relationship with her boyfriend during the early sessions of her therapy, Alice continued to feel increasingly that he was self-centered and preoccupied with himself. He only wanted to talk about his work, she said, and was not interested in her activities. She described how she felt neglected and mistreated and became furious with him. Her relationship with the therapist generally felt supportive to her, but on several occasions when the therapist focused on how she felt about herself when she was ignored, the patient felt that he was implying that her experience with her boyfriend was not real and that she was fabricating it. At these times she would become angry with the therapist and insist that he was interested in proving some theory of his own and did not really want to understand her. The therapist would then return to her experience and clarify that she did not feel he was on her side and that she needed him to understand how difficult her boyfriend was for her. She was able at times to understand that her relationship with her boyfriend automatically revived her childhood feeling of not being valued as a female, and that this feeling reinforced and fueled her anger at him. She did decide to stop seeing him about nine months after starting treatment, and this was very difficult for her as she began to ruminate about how she might have been more appealing to him. In particular, she focused on her physical attributes and her overall feeling that she was unattractive. The therapist clarified for her again how she organized the meaning of this experience according to her own feeling of deficiency. It revived for her the recurrent and painful feelings associated with her father's rejecting her because she was a girl.

As she began to feel better about her decision, a pattern began to take form in the transference. Alice began increasingly to focus on the therapist as a source of romantic interest. This occurred gradually but with greater intensity over a period of several months. The patient was embarrassed at first but indicated that she found the therapist attractive and wanted to meet a man just like him. She told him she was concerned that he would be uncomfortable with her and that he would pull away. Assimilating the patient's concerns into an organizing principle of his own, the therapist reassured her that he would not withdraw from her. He also communicated his understanding that her feelings represented a longing to consolidate and build a sense of herself as a female, as this had never happened in her family. Soon the patient's romantic interest became tinged with sexual fantasy. She confided that she had sexual dreams involving the therapist but said she was too embarrassed to describe the details. She began to ask for a more direct responsiveness from the therapist. She said she could sense that he found her attractive, and she felt certain of this. The therapist acknowledged how important it was that she feel special to him. On a few occasions she would respond angrily and say that she knew he felt she was unique and that she was upset that he would not directly confirm this. The therapist, now in the grip of a conflict within himself, replied equivocally, stating that she was indeed a special person and that she needed to feel this about herself.

After being in therapy for 18 months, the patient was away for an eight-week trip in which she took a group of children on a cultural tour of several foreign countries. When she returned she was happy and excited about what she had done but acutely felt the absence of a man who might share her excitement with her. She had thought of the therapist often during the trip and had fantasized about the two of them enjoying the beauty together. As she began to tell the therapist about a present she had purchased for him, he reacted uneasily and told her that it was not necessary for her to give him a gift. The patient was crestfallen and then became angry. She felt that the therapist had completely rejected her and that, although he had previously encouraged a special relationship with him, he was now changing his attitude. She felt he had misled her, and she said that she would seriously consider finding a new therapist.

During the next few sessions the patient expressed an intense need for the therapist to indicate directly that he found her attractive and sexually exciting. Her demands for a concrete affirmation of her sexual self became increasingly strident. The therapist, feeling enormous pressure, finally did acknowledge that she was an attractive woman whom many men would find appealing. The patient became furious at what she felt was a lukewarm response. She continued to demand that he simply acknowledge that he felt sexually excited by her. She reiterated her awareness that they would actually never do anything sexually, but she still wanted him to demonstrate that he was interested and excited. In reaction to her increasing demands, the therapist became more emotionally disengaged and, adopting a more intellectual stance, asked why she was feeling so needy at this time. The patient became even more incensed and felt that he was abandoning her and that she should leave him. It was at this point that the therapist sought consultation in an attempt to understand what had happened between them.

As a result of the consultation it became clear that an intense stalemate had developed from the interaction between the patient's and therapist's organizing principles. The patient's invariant principle was that no man would ever sustain an interest in her as a female. This was the product of her repeated experience of her father being totally uninterested in her because she was not male. She had mobilized with the therapist an intense developmental longing for mirroring responsiveness to her femaleness—a longing that had become eroticized. The therapist had attempted to be flexible in response to the patient's needs.

His efforts to be responsive, however, had been codetermined by an archaic organizing principle of his own. As a child he had felt required to devote himself to maintaining his mother's self-esteem by mirroring her for her physical attributes. In addition, his mother would periodically become enraged at him because of some slight he had inflicted. Although these episodes were infrequent, they were very frightening and powerful for him. It became absolutely imperative for him to anticipate what would make his mother angry and to avoid this at any cost. In the treatment situation, the patient's intense need for mirroring of her sexual attractiveness, together with her propensity to become enraged when injured, had revived these painful themes from the therapist's history. His self-esteem became focused on maintaining the patient's emotional equilibrium, instead of investigating and elucidating her inner experience. The patient's demands had become assimilated into an archaic organizing principle of the therapist that required him literally and concretely to fulfill the patient's longings for affirmation and to prevent her from reexperiencing with him the painful developmental failures of her childhood. However, continuing along the path of direct fulfillment had increasingly put the therapist into conflict with his personal ideals as an analyst. Thus the therapist had been ambiguous in his message to the patient around her developing sense of femininity. While at times he concretely affirmed her in an attempt to be responsive and extend his own boundaries, at other times he became alarmed about the potential consequences of his responsiveness and the patient's escalating demands and then withdrew into cool intellectualization.

In the next several sessions the therapist conveyed to Alice his understanding of their interaction and how it had unfolded. He communicated to her that he had tried to extend his range of interactions with her in an attempt to be responsive to her needs. She was, however, perceiving and reacting to his oscillation between a responsive mirroring stance and a retreat into more distant intellectual inquiry, which made her feel like a specimen. He stated that at this point he wanted to establish a firmer definition of his own boundaries so that he could help restore a therapeutic atmosphere between them. He told her that his ideal of himself as an analyst prevented him from responding directly to her questions about whether he found her sexually attractive and exciting. He acknowledged that because of a conflict within himself—between a feeling that he must be responsive to her and an equally strong feeling that he must live up to his own analytic ideals—he had sometimes withdrawn from her, as when he had rejected her gift. He said that, within the limits of his own view of himself as an analyst, he would like to work with her to reestablish their relationship. The patient responded very favorably. She said that, although she thought his training was somewhat stupid, she understood what had happened and now had an idea of what she could expect. She indicated, upon inquiry, that she did *not* experience the analyst's new stance as a recoiling from her because she was unappealing sexually, nor did she renounce her feelings and wishes.

Clarifying the intersubjective disjunction both reestablished a facilitating atmosphere between therapist and patient and made possible a deepening understanding of the principles organizing the patient's experience in the transference. The patient continued to have romantic feelings toward the therapist, but the demands for a concrete response receded. Concomitantly, the patient became aware of her underlying conviction that the therapist must surely be repulsed by her romantic and erotic feelings. Alice and the therapist came to understand that her central and most painful fear in the transference was not that she would be rejected as sexually unattractive, but that her *feelings* and *longings* for responsiveness in and of themselves would repel and alienate the therapist. This fear was accompanied by a belief that he must feel dirtied and disgusted by his association with her and that he must be relieved when she left his office. Thus, the successful illumination of the impasse had unveiled the patient's deep conviction that her affective longings were repugnant, a sign of a loathsome defect within herself. This conviction, along with its childhood roots, could then become a primary focus of analytic investigation.

For the therapist, the new understanding of his own vulnerabilities and the firmer delineation to the patient of his analytic ideals created an increased sense of confidence. The patient's feelings of disappointment and anger could then be seen as an inevitable component of the process of her consolidating her sense of herself as a female, not as a harbinger of a disaster that he had to forestall. The clarification of the intersubjective disjunction freed him of the requirement that he concentrate on alleviating her distress and helped create an atmosphere wherein he felt a greater freedom to be naturally responsive from within a stance of sustained empathic inquiry.

The Case of Sarah

Sarah, a 27-year-old unmarried physical therapist entered treatment because of recurring experiences of herself as a small, vulnerable child lost in a threatening world of powerful grown-ups. She was in actuality a successful, well-respected professional, with many supervisees and disabled patients relying on her expertise. Subjectively, however, she was increasingly prey to feelings of extreme intimidation, as if she were a weak and inadequate little girl suddenly thrust into high-powered adult roles and responsibilities.

Sarah had made one earlier attempt at psychotherapy while she was in college, but this had ended disastrously after two years when her therapist began to use her for the fulfillment of his own sexual needs. She was devastated when, after finally expressing confusion and doubt concerning their physical intimacy, he angrily told her that he had made a mistake in believing she had become capable of "mature love." Never showing any understanding of her reactions, he made her feel completely deserted by him. The final result of this was that she resolved never to rely so deeply on another person again and tried to block the entire episode out of her mind for the next several years.

A pattern of being emotionally neglected and exploited actually was characteristic of her whole life history. During her early years there was massive neglect by her depressed and alcoholic parents, who for the most part relied on her to take care of them. Being nurturant to the parents provided the only consistent means of experiencing a connection with them, and major aspects of her developing self became organized around the caregiving role. This role specifically excluded showing any direct need for care from her mother or father; expressing such a need seemed invariably to make the parents resentful, and they reacted either by pressuring her to be grown-up or by angrily rejecting her for being a burden to them. Illustrative of this pattern were the patient's earliest memories, which were of times when she cried uncontrollably in her crib and her mother responded by screaming at her to be quiet and violently throwing a bottle into her bedding.

Among the long-range consequences of Sarah's early situation was an interpersonal style of giving to others but asking nothing directly for herself. This style affected not only her career choice in the field of disability, but also her intimate relationships. Her history was one of a series of romances in which she played a nurturant role with men who gave little or nothing in return. She always reacted to the depriving quality of these relationships with upset and depression but regarded such feelings as signs of something wrong with her rather than reflections of how she was being mistreated.

The first months of Sarah's new therapy seemed to unfold very smoothly. She told the long story of her life in all its sad detail, including the story of her relationship to her first therapist. Her new therapist listened sympathetically as she spoke, and, although he noted the rapidity with which she seemed to be opening up the various areas of her experience, he did not anticipate the transference storms that were soon to arise. There was an early dream, symbolizing the process that was occurring, in which the patient traveled back to the town where she had grown up, approached a large house and went in. She passed through room after room and finally came to a small closet in which an infant covered with dirt, cuts, and bruises cowered against the wall. In discussing the dream, she and her therapist understood the imagery as a picturing of their developing discovery of the sequestered, deeply hurt child within her.

The impasse to be described crystalized around the therapist's telling Sarah of a six-week interruption in their work that was to occur during the following summer. Recognizing that such a long separation might be exceptionally difficult for her, he explained that he would be only a phone call away. She showed no special reaction to the announcement for a few days but then reported a dream of an old mangy animal left lying on its back in the wilderness. When her therapist suggested that perhaps the dream was related to his plans for the summer, she grew visibly frightened, haltingly saying that maybe she was experiencing an impending abandonment. At this point the therapist repeated his reassurances that he could remain in touch with her by phone and reminded her they still had a number of months to decide how they would handle the separation. To his surprise, Sarah reacted to the intended reassurance by becoming still more upset and turning physically away from him. When asked what she had felt, she said that she could not bear being in the room for a moment longer and wanted to go home. Her therapist asked her not to leave, but rather to stay and tell him more of what she was feeling. Again she responded fearfully and was now unable to talk. The session continued essentially in a tense silence until the hour was finally over, at which point Sarah rushed out the door.

The patient now began coming late to their meetings, reported great difficulty restraining herself from running away once she had arrived, and otherwise had little to say. The therapist redoubled his efforts to understand the meaning of the impending separation and continued to seek ways to ameliorate its inexplicably growing disruptive impact. He told the patient he was sure they could find their way through this period by planning for it and having occasional contacts by telephone, and he even offered to see her once during the middle of the six-week interruption when he had to return briefly. With each of these efforts to explore and soften the effect of his departure, Sarah became still more frightened and unable to communicate her feelings to him. She then told of recurring nightmares in which she arrived at his building for a session, but somehow his office had vanished and she was unable to find him. As the situation worsened, the therapist began to feel more and more helpless, at times becoming consumed with anxiety on her behalf. Sarah noted her therapist's growing distress, and this added to her difficulties, for now she felt she had become a painful burden to him.

During the vacation itself, the patient refused to have ongoing contacts of any kind and rejected her therapist's calls with what he experienced as icy hostility. Finally she sent a letter telling him that he had treated her with brutal insensitivity. She added that she felt completely betrayed by him and was therefore terminating treatment. Still not understanding what had transpired, he replied in writing that he regretted the ending of their relationship and hoped she would feel welcome to come back if she ever changed her mind. Sarah did finally return after several more weeks had passed, and their sessions continued. The impasse, however, persisted through a series of subsequent episodes and was only very slowly clarified over the next 18 months. These episodes had in common a crisis around a physical separation interrupting their work or some other circumstance dramatizing an aspect of the therapist's unavailability to the patient. In each instance Sarah again reacted to her therapist's attempts to understand and alleviate her pain by withdrawing, and the treatment was maintained during this interval only on the most precarious basis.

The illumination of the impasse occurred gradually and involved not only a new understanding of the patient, but also a concomitant change in the therapist's self-understanding. For Sarah, the crises pertained most fundamentally to her sense that her therapist showed no concern for the enormously frightened, vulnerable child she repeatedly experienced herself as being. His attempted reassurances that a way could be found to overcome the disruptions of occasional separations she perceived as implicit demands that she feel better and not become scared. This replicated early childhood scenes in which her parents expected her to withstand very trying circumstances, including sometimes long separations from them, and behave like the grown-up girl they needed her to be. Her first therapist as well had told her that he expected her to be "mature" and made her feel that she had lost all connection to him on account of her failure to do so. A fundamental truth of Sarah's life was that she had never been allowed to be a child, and with her new therapist she was again experiencing the same disastrous situation. His expectation that she join with him in planning for a separation flew in the face of her feeling that such a long break in their contacts was utterly impossible to bear. What was most disruptive for her was not, it was later understood, the six-week separation itself; the more central problem was that she felt that her therapist could neither understand nor accept the paralyzing sadness and despair his departure was triggering. His well-meaning efforts to arrange contacts to help her only dramatized this lack of understanding. She also had been experiencing his efforts as containing the implicit message that she should not be so upset, and thus as a rejection of her child-self. This self had originally been disavowed in consequence of repeated events making her believe that the expression of her needs threatened her ties to the people closest to her. The specific danger associated with the emergence of her long-suppressed childhood longing for understanding and loving care was that she would be rejected for imposing such a loathsome burden on anyone around her. This danger had seemed actually to materialize when her therapist first informed her of his summer plans.

Throughout the period of the impasse the therapist did not clearly perceive the patient's child-self as a distinct part of her. He was aware of her intense suffering but did not fully comprehend the nature of this suffering as the boundless despair of a small child. Instead he tended to see the difficulty she was having in terms of the relationship between them and felt responsible for her pain. This feeling of magnified responsibility contributed to his intense distress and formed part of a vicious cycle by reinforcing her picture of herself as an intrinsically burdensome, rotten creature that no one could ever love.

The changes in the therapist's self-understanding that contributed to the resolution of the impasse arose largely out of his personal analysis, which was occurring in parallel to the treatment being described. He was a person in whom there was also a disavowed child-self, but with a background different from that of his patient. He had grown up in a family that had been profoundly affected by the sudden death of his mother when he was eight years old. She had been the emotional center of family life, and her loss had been utterly shattering to all the family members. The therapist had as a child responded to this massive upheaval in part by forming an identification with his mother and assuming aspects of her nurturant, supporting role in relation to his grieving father and siblings. His own sense of inner desolation was hidden in this process, becoming buried, as it

were, with his mother. The result was that much of his style of
relating to others began to center on the themes of caretaking
and rescue, which served to protect him from feelings of devastating powerlessness and solitude. His inability to rescue Sarah
as she spiraled into despair had thus challenged a central part of
his way of maintaining his own emotional equilibrium.

As a result of intensive analytic work, the therapist began to
have the immediate experience of his own child-self, with all its
attendant feelings. The gradual integration of this previously
disavowed part of himself occurred within the bond to *his* analyst, which provided elements of the holding, containing context that had been missing in the shattered family of his youth.
A central theme in his analysis was in fact the recognition of
how he had been hurt not only by the loss of his mother, but
equally by the emotional unavailability into which his father
and other family members had lapsed in the aftermath of her
death. As this integration slowly took place, his perception of
his patient also began to change. He now came to see her
child-self as a much more distinct entity than had been apparent
to him before. He understood also that within this part of her
there was an indescribable depth of despair and loneliness, feelings that again and again had been triggered in the transference.
He specifically grasped why all his efforts to ease Sarah's pain
during their separations had failed: the separations were simply
impossible for the child within her to manage, and she had
needed from him a response showing his understanding and
acceptance of this fact. His efforts to reassure her contained the
expectation that she would do well while he was away, which
was very far from how she felt. This expectation had made it
seem that he was no longer available for contact with her, and
this was symbolized in the dreams of his office having disappeared. The reassurances were in addition felt as rejections of
her child-self, rejections that replicated the many traumatic interactions with her parents and first therapist.

With the therapist's increasing acceptance and tolerance of the
catastrophically extreme emotions of his own childhood, he
became able to tolerate and contain the correspondingly extreme
feelings of his patient. No longer assimilating the circumstances
of the treatment to the trauma of his early family situation, he

no longer felt a compelling need to rescue his patient from her pain and despair. As he moved away from attempts to ameliorate her suffering and focused instead on conveying his understanding of what she felt, Sarah slowly began to relax in his presence. The changing intersubjective field then made it possible for her to tell of a wishful fantasy concerning what she most deeply yearned for from him, a fantasy that previously she would have been far too frightened to disclose. It was that she could be held protectively in her therapist's arms and fall gradually into a peaceful sleep. This imagery concretized a needed bond that was at this point crystallizing between them, a bond of holding and containment within which the patient could experience secure acceptance of her child-self and thus discover the possibility of her own emotional wholeness.

DISCUSSION

We presented two brief clinical examples (the cases of Peter and Robyn) in which, in the absence of reflective self-awareness on the part of the therapist, patterns of intersubjective transaction became established that resulted in unresolved therapeutic stalemates. In contrast, we offered two more extensive clinical reports (the cases of Alice and Sarah) illustrating our thesis that when the principles unconsciously organizing the experiences of patient and therapist in an impasse can be investigated and illuminated, significant new understandings and enhancements of the therapeutic process can be achieved.

The cases of Robyn and Alice are similar in that, for both patients, early unmet developmental needs for mirroring responsiveness took on a sexualized form when these needs were revived but then rebuffed by the therapists. Robyn's therapist remained unaware of the psychological configuration that led him to reject his patient's longings, with the result that the erotization of the transference became hopelessly entrenched. Alice's therapist, in contrast, became reflectively aware of his unconscious organizing activity, in turn making it possible to open up for investigation the more primary emotional constellation underlying his patient's eroticized demands.

The cases of Peter and Sarah are similar in that in both instances an overlap between areas of the patient's and the therapist's defensive activity opposed the process of analytic investigation. Unlike Peter's therapist, however, Sarah's therapist worked through the defensive disavowal of painful childhood feelings in his own analysis, enabling him to make empathic contact with the traumatized child-self sequestered within his patient.

In the cases of both Alice and Sarah, their therapists' attainment of reflective self-awareness permitted them to recognize and comprehend the intersubjective disjunctions and conjunctions that had produced the therapeutic impasses. There was, however, an important difference in the manner in which the impasses were resolved in these two instances. Alice's therapist disclosed to his patient aspects of his own psychological world that had contributed to the impasse. This disclosure proved highly facilitative because, by revealing himself to be torn between his wish to be responsive and his wish to uphold his ideals, he distinguished himself from the dreaded father, who had recoiled from Alice because she was female. In contrast, Sarah's therapist wisely refrained from revealing to her what he had discovered about the disavowals of his own childhood pain that had interfered with his capacity to comprehend her child-self, for she doubtlessly would have experienced such a disclosure as a replication of her parents' expectation that she disregard her own distress and devote herself to nurturing them. What the therapist may or may not reveal about his own contribution to an impasse should be guided by his understanding of the specific transference meanings such disclosures are likely to acquire for the patient.

We (Stolorow et al., 1987) have argued that the analytic stance is best conceptualized as an attitude of sustained empathic inquiry. What we are emphasizing here is that inquiry must include the therapist's continual reflection on the involvement of his own personal subjectivity in the ongoing therapeutic process. Since the patient's experience of the therapeutic relationship is codetermined by the organizing activities of both participants in the therapeutic dialogue, the domain of analytic investigation must encompass the entire intersubjective field created by the interplay between the subjective worlds of patient and therapist. As we have seen, an investigation conducted in this manner can transform a therapeutic stalemate into a royal road to new analytic understandings for both patient and therapist.

Epilogue

THE DOCTRINE OF THE ISOLATED MIND in psychoanalysis has historically been associated with an objectivist epistemology. Such a position envisions the mind in isolation, radically estranged from an external reality that it either accurately apprehends or distorts. Analysts embracing an objectivist epistemology presume to have privileged access to the essence of the patient's psychic reality and to the objective truths that the patient's psychic reality obscures. In contrast, the intersubjective viewpoint, emphasizing the constitutive interplay between worlds of experience, leads inevitably to an epistemological stance that is best characterized as "perspectivalist" (Rorty, 1989; Orange, 1992). Such a stance does not presume either that the analyst's subjective reality is more true than the patient's, or that the analyst can directly know the subjective reality of the patient. In contrast with a radically relativist position, which denies the existence of a psychic reality that can be known, a perspectivalist stance assumes the existence of the patient's psychic reality but claims only to be able to approximate this reality from within the particularized scope of the analyst's own perspective (cf. Hoffman, 1991).

We wish to emphasize that we are not enjoining analysts to refrain from using guiding theoretical ideas to order clinical data.

Instead, we are claiming that analysts should recognize the impact of their guiding frameworks in both delimiting their grasp of their patients' subjective worlds and in codetermining the course of the analytic process, an impact that must itself become a subject of analytic investigation.

We are led inexorably to a consideration of the limits of self-reflection. How can an analyst be expected to reflect on the nature and impact of his own organizing principles, including especially those enshrined in his theoretical perspective, when his acts of self-reflection will be shaped by the very principles whose nature and impact he seeks to comprehend? Analysts are in the position of the mythical snake devouring itself by swallowing its own tail unless they are able to reflect from a position that encompasses principles of organization alternative to the ones being reflected upon. It would be difficult for us, for example, to reflect fully on the particularizing impact of our principle of intersubjectivity, insofar as this is the central constituent of our analytic perspective. It must be left to others to integrate our contributions within a still more general and inclusive viewpoint.

References

Abraham, K. (1919), A particular form of neurotic resistance against the psychoanalytic method. In: *Selected Papers of Karl Abraham, M.D.* London: Hogarth Press, 1927, pp. 303–311.

Arlow, J. (1969), Unconscious fantasy and disturbances of conscious experience. *Psychoanal. Quart.*, 38:1–27.

Atwood, G. & Stolorow, R. (1984), *Structures of Subjectivity: Explorations in Psychoanalytic Phenomenology.* Hillsdale, NJ: The Analytic Press.

Bacal, H. & Newman, K. (1990), *Theories of Object Relations.* New York: Columbia University Press.

Balint, M. (1969), Trauma and object relationship. *Internat. J. Psycho-Anal.*, 50:429–435.

Barrett, W. (1979), *The Illusion of Technique.* New York: Doubleday.

Basch, M. (1984), Selfobjects and selfobject transference. In: *Kohut's Legacy,* ed. P. Stepansky & A. Goldberg. Hillsdale, NJ: The Analytic Press, pp. 21–41.

_____ (1988), *Understanding Psychotherapy.* New York: Basic Books.

Becker, E. (1973), *The Denial of Death.* New York: The Free Press.

_____ (1975), *Escape From Evil.* New York: The Free Press.

Beebe, B., Jaffe, J., & Lachmann, F. (1992), A dyadic systems view of communication. In: *Relational Perspectives in Psychoanalysis,* ed. N. Skolnick & S. Warshaw. Hillsdale, NJ: The Analytic Press.

———— & Lachmann, F. (1988a), The contribution of mother-infant mutual influence to the origins of self- and object representations. *Psychoanal. Psychol.,* 5:305–337.

———— ———— (1988b), Mother-infant mutual influence and precursors of psychic structure. In: *Frontiers in Self Psychology: Progress in Self Psychology, Vol. 4,* ed. A. Goldberg. Hillsdale, NJ: The Analytic Press, pp. 3–25.

Bibring, E. (1937), On the theory of the results of psychoanalysis. *Internat. J. Psycho-Anal.,* 18:170–189.

Brandchaft, B. (1983), The negativism of the negative therapeutic reaction and the psychology of the self. In: *The Future of Psychoanalysis,* ed. A. Goldberg. Madison, CT: International Universities Press, pp. 327–359.

———— (1991), To free the spirit from its cell. Presented at the Fourteenth Annual Conference on the Psychology of the Self, Chicago, October 11.

———— & Stolorow, R. (1984), The borderline concept: Pathological character or iatrogenic myth? In: *Empathy II,* ed. J. Lichtenberg, M. Bornstein & D. Silver. Hillsdale, NJ: The Analytic Press, pp. 333–357.

———— ———— (1990), Varieties of therapeutic alliance. *The Annual of Psychoanalysis,* 18:99–114. Hillsdale, NJ: The Analytic Press.

Breuer, J. & Freud, S. (1893–95). Studies on hysteria. *Standard Edition, 2.* London: Hogarth Press, 1955.

Bromberg, P. (1991), On knowing one's patient inside out. *Psychoanal. Dial.,* 1:399–422.

Demos, E. V. (1988), Affect and the development of the self. In: *Frontiers in Self Psychology: Progress in Self Psychology, Vol. 4,* ed. A. Goldberg. Hillsdale, NJ: The Analytic Press, pp. 27–53.

———— & Kaplan, S. (1986), Motivation and affect reconsidered. *Psychoanal. Contemp. Thought,* 9:147–221.

Emde, R. (1988a), Development terminable and interminable: I. *Internat. J. Psycho-Anal.,* 69:23–42.

_____ (1988b), Development terminable and interminable: II. *Internat. J. Psycho-Anal.,* 69:283–296.

Fairbairn, W. (1943). The repression and the return of bad objects. In: *Psychoanalytic Studies of the Personality.* London: Routledge & Kegan Paul, 1952, pp. 59–81.

_____ (1952). *Psychoanalytic Studies of the Personality.* London: Routledge & Kegan Paul.

Fenichel, O. (1941). *Problems of Psychoanalytic Technique.* Albany, NY: Psychoanalytic Quarterly.

_____ (1945), *The Psychoanalytic Theory of Neurosis.* New York: Norton.

Ferenczi, S. (1913), Stages in the development of the sense of reality. In: *Sex in Psychoanalysis.* Boston: Badger, 1916, pp. 213–239.

_____ (1933), Confusion of tongues between adults and the child. In: *Final Contributions to the Problems and Methods of Psycho-Analysis.* London: Hogarth Press, pp. 156–167.

Freud, S. (1895), Project for a scientific psychology. *Standard Edition,* 1:294–387. London: Hogarth Press, 1950.

_____ (1900), The interpretation of dreams. *Standard Edition,* 4 & 5. London: Hogarth Press, 1953.

_____ (1905), Three essays on the theory of sexuality. *Standard Edition,* 7:135–243. London: Hogarth Press, 1953.

_____ (1914), On the history of the psycho-analytic movement. *Standard Edition,* 14:7–66. London: Hogarth Press, 1957.

_____ (1915), The unconscious. *Standard Edition,* 14:159–204. London: Hogarth Press, 1957.

_____ (1917), Mourning and melancholia. *Standard Edition,* 14:239–258. London: Hogarth Press, 1957.

_____ (1923), The ego and the id. *Standard Edition,* 19:3–66. London: Hogarth Press, 1961.

_____ (1926), Inhibitions, symptoms, and anxiety. *Standard Edition,* 20:77–175. London: Hogarth Press, 1959.

_____ (1937), Analysis terminable and interminable. *Standard Edition,* 23:211–253. London: Hogarth Press, 1964.

Goldberg, A. (1975), A fresh look at perverse behavior. *Internat. J. Psycho-Anal.,* 56:335–342.

Greenacre, P. (1958), Toward an understanding of the physical nucleus of some defense mechanisms. *Internat. J. Psycho-Anal.*, 39:69–76.

Greenson, R. (1954), The struggle against identification. *J. Amer. Psychoanal. Assn.*, 2:200–217.

——— (1967), *The Technique and Practice of Psychoanalysis.* Madison, CT: International Universities Press.

Hartmann, H. (1939), *Ego Psychology and the Problem of Adaptation.* Madison, CT: International Universities Press, 1958.

Hoffer, W. (1950), Development of the body ego. *The Psychoanalytic Study of the Child,* 5:18–23. Madison, CT: International Universities Press.

——— (1952), The mutual influences in the development of the ego and the id. *The Psychoanalytic Study of the Child,* 7:31–41. Madison, CT: International Universities Press.

Hoffman, I. (1991), Discussion: Toward a social-constructivist view of the psychoanalytic situation. *Psychoanal. Dial.,* 1:74–105.

Jacobson, E. (1964), *The Self and the Object World.* Madison, CT: International Universities Press.

Jones, J. (in press). *Affects as Process.* Hillsdale, NJ: The Analytic Press.

Joseph, B. (1982), Addiction to near-death. *Internat. J. Psycho-Anal.,* 63:449–456.

Kernberg, O. (1975), *Borderline Conditions and Pathological Narcissism.* Northvale, NJ: Aronson.

——— (1976), *Object Relations Theory and Clinical Psychoanalysis.* Northvale, NJ: Aronson.

——— (1982), Review of *Advances in Self Psychology. Amer. J. Psychiat.,* 139:374–375.

——— (1987), Projection and projective identification. *J. Amer. Psychoanal. Assn.,* 35:795–819.

Khan, M. (1963), The concept of cumulative trauma. In: *The Privacy of the Self.* Madison, CT: International Universities Press, 1974, pp. 42–58.

Klein, M. (1940), Mourning and its relation to manic-depressive states. In: *Contributions to Psycho-Analysis 1921–1945.* London: Hogarth Press, 1950, pp. 311–338.

——— (1950), *Contributions to Psycho-Analysis 1921–1945.* London: Hogarth Press.

_____ (1957), Envy and gratitude. In: *Envy and Gratitude and Other Works 1946-1963.* New York: Delta, 1977, pp. 176-235.

_____ (1961), *Narrative of a Child Analysis.* New York: Basic Books.

Kohut, H. (1959), Introspection, empathy, and psychoanalysis. In: *The Search for the Self, Vol. 1,* ed. P. Ornstein. Madison, CT: International Universities Press, 1978, pp. 205-232.

_____ (1971), *The Analysis of the Self.* Madison, CT: International Universities Press.

_____ (1977), *The Restoration of the Self.* Madison, CT: International Universities Press.

_____ (1982), Introspection, empathy, and the semicircle of mental health. *Internat. J. Psycho-Anal.,* 63:395-407.

_____ (1984), *How Does Analysis Cure?* ed. A. Goldberg and P. Stepansky. Chicago: University of Chicago Press.

Kramer, S. & Akhtar, S. (eds.) (1991), *The Trauma of Transgression.* Northvale, NJ: Aronson.

Kris, E. (1956), The recovery of childhood memories in psychoanalysis. *The Psychoanalytic Study of the Child,* 11:54-88. Madison, CT: International Universities Press.

Krueger, D. (1989), *Body Self and Psychological Self.* New York: Brunner/Mazel.

Krystal, H. (1988), *Integration and Self-Healing: Affect, Trauma, Alexithymia.* Hillsdale, NJ: The Analytic Press.

Kundera, M. (1984), *The Unbearable Lightness of Being.* New York: Harper & Row.

Lacan, J. (1949), The mirror stage as formative of the function of the I as revealed in psychoanalytic experience. In: *Ecrits.* New York: Norton, 1977, pp. 1-7.

_____ (1953), The function and field of speech and language in psychoanalysis. In: *Ecrits.* New York: Norton, 1977, pp. 30-113.

Laing, R. D. (1960), *The Divided Self.* London: Pelican, 1965.

Lee, R. (1988), Reverse selfobject experience. *Amer. J. Psychother.,* 42:416-424.

Levine, H. (ed.) (1990), *Adult Analysis and Childhood Sexual Abuse.* Hillsdale, NJ: The Analytic Press.

Lichtenberg, J. (1983), *Psychoanalysis and Infant Research.* Hillsdale, NJ: The Analytic Press.

———— (1989), *Psychoanalysis and Motivation.* Hillsdale, NJ: The Analytic Press.

Lifton, R. (1976), *The Life of the Self.* New York: Simon & Schuster.

Mahler, M., Pine, F., & Bergman, A. (1975), *The Psychological Birth of the Human Infant.* New York: Basic Books.

Matson, F. (1964), *The Broken Image.* New York: Doubleday.

McDougall, J. (1989), *Theaters of the Body.* New York: Norton.

Mijuscovic, B. (1988), *Loneliness.* Chicago: Libra.

Miller, A. (1986), *Thou Shalt Not Be Aware.* New York: New American Library.

Mitchell, S. (1988), *Relational Concepts in Psychoanalysis.* Cambridge, MA: Harvard University Press.

Modell, A. (1976), The "holding environment" and the therapeutic action of psychoanalysis. *J. Amer. Psychoanal. Assn.,* 24:285–307.

Ogden, T. (1991), Some theoretical comments on personal isolation. *Psychoanal. Dial.,* 1:377–390.

Orange, D. (1992), Subjectivism, relativism, and realism in psychoanalysis. In: *New Therapeutic Visions: Progress in Self Psychology, Vol. 8,* ed. A. Goldberg. Hillsdale, NJ: The Analytic Press, pp. 189–197.

Ornstein, A. (1974), The dread to repeat and the new beginning. *The Annual of Psychoanalysis,* 2:231–248. Madison, CT: International Universities Press.

Rank, O. (1930), *Psychology and the Soul.* New York: Barnes, 1961.

Riviere, J. (1936), A contribution to the analysis of the negative therapeutic reaction. *Internat. J. Psycho-Anal.,* 17:304–320.

Rogawski, A. (1987), A systems theoretical approach to the understanding of emotions. *J. Amer. Acad. Psychoanal.,* 15:133–151.

Rorty, R. (1989), *Contingency, Irony, and Solidarity.* Cambridge: Cambridge University Press.

Rosenfeld, H. (1987), Destructive narcissism. In: *Impasse and Interpretation.* New York: Routledge, pp. 105–133.

Rubinstein, B. (1976), On the possibility of a strictly clinical

psychoanalytic theory. In: *Psychology Versus Metapsychology,*
ed. M. Gill & P. Holzman. Madison, CT: International
Universities Press, pp. 229–264.

Sander, L. (1985), Toward a logic of organization in psycho-
biological development. In: *Biologic Response Styles,* ed. H.
Klar & L. Siever. Washington, DC: American Psychiatric
Ass., pp. 20–36.

———— (1987), Awareness of inner experience. *Child Abuse &
Neglect,* 11:339–346.

———— (1991), Recognition process. Presented at conference on
the Psychic Life of the Infant, University of Massachusetts,
Amherst, June 28–30.

Schafer, R. (1976), *A New Language for Psychoanalysis.* New Ha-
ven, CT: Yale University Press.

Schwaber, E. (1983), Psychoanalytic listening and psychic reality. *Internat. Rev. Psycho-Anal.,* 10:379–392.

———— (1984), Empathy. In: *Empathy II,* ed. J. Lichtenberg, M.
Bornstein & D. Silver. Hillsdale, NJ: The Analytic Press,
pp. 143–172.

Shabad, P. (1989), Vicissitudes of psychic loss of a physically
present parent. In: *The Problem of Loss and Mourning,* ed. D.
Dietrich & P. Shabad. Madison, CT: International Universities Press, pp. 101–126.

Shane, E. & Shane, M. (1990), Object loss and selfobject loss.
The Annual of Psychoanalysis, 18:115–131. Hillsdale, NJ: The
Analytic Press.

Slap, J. (1987), Implications for the structural model of Freud's
assumptions about perception. *J. Amer. Psychanal. Assn.,*
35:629–645.

Socarides, C. (1988), *The Preoedipal Origin and Psychoanalytic
Therapy of Sexual Perversions.* Madison, CT: International
Universities Press.

Socarides, D. D. & Stolorow, R. (1984/85), Affects and selfobjects. *The Annual of Psychoanalysis,* 12/13:105–119. Madison,
CT: International Universities Press.

Sterba, R. (1934), The fate of the ego in analytic therapy. *Internat. J. Psycho-Anal.,* 15:117–126.

Stern, D. (1985), *The Interpersonal World of the Infant.* New York:
Basic Books.

_____ (1988), The dialectic between the "interpersonal" and the "intrapsychic." *Psychoanal. Inq.*, 8:505–512.

Stolorow, D. S. & Stolorow, R. (1989), My brother's keeper: Intensive treatment of a case of delusional merger. *Internat. J. Psycho-Anal.*, 70:315–326.

Stolorow, R. (1989), The dream in context. In: *Dimensions of Self Experience: Progress in Self Psychology, Vol. 5,* ed. A. Goldberg. Hillsdale, NJ: The Analytic Press, pp. 33–39.

_____ (1992), Subjectivity and self psychology: A personal odyssey. In: *New Therapeutic Visions: Progress in Self Psychology, Vol. 8,* ed. A. Goldberg. Hillsdale, NJ: The Analytic Press, pp. 241–250.

_____ (in press), Thoughts on the nature and therapeutic action of psychoanalytic interpretation. In: *Progress in Self Psychology, Vol. 9,* ed. A. Goldberg. Hillsdale, NJ: The Analytic Press.

_____ & Atwood, G. (1979), *Faces in a Cloud: Subjectivity in Personality Theory.* Northvale, NJ: Aronson.

_____ _____ & Brandchaft, B. (1992), Three realms of the unconscious and their therapeutic transformation. *Psychoanal. Rev.*, 79:25–30.

_____ _____ & Ross, J. (1978), The representational world in psychoanalytic therapy. *Internat. Rev. Psycho-Anal.*, 5:247–256.

_____ & Brandchaft, B. (1987), Developmental failure and psychic conflict. *Psychoanal. Psychol.*, 4:241–253.

_____ _____ & Atwood, G. (1983), Intersubjectivity in psychoanalytic treatment: With special reference to archaic states. *Bull. Menninger Clin.*, 47:117–128.

_____ _____ _____ (1987), *Psychoanalytic Treatment: An Intersubjective Approach.* Hillsdale, NJ: The Analytic Press.

_____ & Lachmann, F. (1980), *Psychoanalysis of Developmental Arrests: Theory and Treatment.* Madison, CT: International Universities Press.

_____ _____ (1984/85), Transference: The future of an illusion. *The Annual of Psychoanalysis,* 12/13:19–37. Madison, CT: International Universities Press.

Stone, L. (1961), *The Psychoanalytic Situation.* Madison, CT: International Universities Press.

Strachey, J. (1934), The nature of the therapeutic action of psycho-analysis. *Internat. J. Psycho-Anal.*, 15:127–159.

Sullivan, H. S. (1953), *The Interpersonal Theory of Psychiatry.* New York: Norton.

Waelder, R. (1960), *Basic Theory of Psychoanalysis.* Madison, CT: International Universities Press.

Wallace, E. (1985), *Historiography and Causation in Psychoanalysis.* Hillsdale, NJ: The Analytic Press.

———— (1988), Mind–body. *J. Nerv. Ment. Dis.*, 176:4–20.

Winnicott, D. W. (1945), Primitive emotional development. In: *Through Paediatrics to Psycho-Analysis.* New York: Basic Books, 1975, pp. 145–156.

———— (1949), Birth memories, birth trauma, and anxiety. In: *Through Paediatrics to Psycho-Analysis.* New York: Basic Books, 1975, pp. 174–193.

———— (1954), Withdrawal and regression. In: *Through Paediatrics to Psycho-Analysis.* New York: Basic Books, 1975, pp. 255–261.

———— (1960), Ego distortion in terms of true and false self. In: *The Maturational Processes and the Facilitating Environment.* Madison, CT: International Universities Press, 1965, pp. 140–152.

———— (1962), Ego integration in child development. In: *The Maturational Processes and the Facilitating Environment.* Madison, CT: International Universities Press, 1965, pp. 56–63.

———— (1963), Psychotherapy of character disorders. In: *The Maturational Processes and the Facilitating Environment.* Madison, CT: International Universities Press, 1965, pp. 203–216.

———— (1967), Mirror-role of mother and family in child development. In: *Playing and Reality.* New York: Basic Books, 1971, pp. 111–118.

Wolf, E. (1979), Transference and countertransference in the analysis of the disorders of the self. *Contemp. Psychoanal.*, 15:577–594.

Zetzel, E. (1956), Current concepts of transference. *Internat. J. Psycho-Anal.*, 37:369–376.

Index